UNDONE

My journey from

abuse and addiction

to freedom

Libby Thompson

Spring View Publications
info@springview.uk

Copyright © Libby Thompson 2025

The right of Libby Thompson to be identified as the author of this work has been asserted by her in accordance with the Copyright, Design and Patents Act 1988.

Unless otherwise indicated, all Scripture quotations are taken from the Holy Bible, New Living Translation, copyright © 1996, 2004, 2015 by Tyndale House Foundation. Used by permission of Tyndale House Publishers, Carol Stream, Illinois 60188. All rights reserved.

Scripture quotations marked The Passion Translation, copyright © 2017, 2018, 2020 by Passion & Fire Ministries, Inc. Used by permission. All rights reserved. ThePassionTranslation.com.

The Chronicles of Narnia by C.S. Lewis copyright © 1950-1956 C.S. Lewis Pte. Ltd. Extracts reprinted by permission.

Cover design by Emma Scott

Typeset by Candy Evans, Kenilworth

Printed and bound by IngramSpark
ingramspark.com

ISBN 978-1-7398659-4-8
ebook ISBN 978-1-7398659-5-5

Acknowledgements	1
Foreword	2
Introduction	4
My family	10
Wanting Dad dead	14
Angel encounter	19
Hitchhiking	22
Mum goes away	24
The final beating	27
Did people know?	29
Prayer	33
Dad leaves – hooray!	35
The assault	37
The Lord makes a way	44
New beginnings	46
Bible College	48
God has a plan	52
Betty	54
The children	56
Miracle-working God	58
Demons in the closet	62
ADHD	68
What a plonker	70
Alcohol addiction grows	72
Sin or addiction – are they the same?	74

The wine witch	76
Set free	82
True repentance	84
My promise to God	87
Piff, paff, puff	89
Life is never easy (but God will help you make the right choices)	94
Phil's story	98
Telling people	106
Let's call a spade a spade	108
The first cut is the deepest	110
Orchestrated	114
Do you know God? Do you want to?	120
The Holy Spirit	126
Pride and deception	129
Alcoholics Anonymous	134
Lead us not into temptation	141
UNDONE	150
For further help	154

Acknowledgements

Thanks so much to God who has enabled all of this to happen, who has given me a life to write about and a future to look forward to.

Thanks, Phil for all you do; I don't know where I would be if God hadn't given you to me. Thanks for all the time you have put into helping me, the proof-reading, editing and for supporting me as I write this book and for being the most wonderful husband I could have ever imagined – my absolute rock of a godly man, my best friend and hero. Thank you for steadfastly loving me, seeing the best in me, never wavering. You are a fantastic husband and dad to our beautiful babies. I love you always and forever.

Thanks Max and Gracie for loving me and sticking with me through all the difficult years of addiction. You are both amazing human beings and I couldn't be prouder of the adults you have both become. I am so blessed to have been given the privilege of being your mum. I love you so much my precious children.

Thanks, Pastor Dave for being our forever friend, for your faithfulness, wisdom and guidance. Thanks for loving me and sticking with me. Thanks for your leadership and for the many spiritual adventures we have been on and the crazy projects we have mastered together. You are an inspirational and great leader. Most importantly, thank you for being my spiritual father and adopting me as your spiritual daughter.

Foreword

Every now and again in our lives we meet someone inspiring who we admire and someone we wish we had some of what they have, in character and perseverance.

I love watching movies where someone 'wins' against all odds, where evil has set itself up against the 'weaker' person, but the 'weaker' person prevails with outright determination, tenacity and a refusal to be defeated.

I love seeing a life where the enemy's plans have been obliterated by the powerful blood of Jesus because they depend on His strength, realising their own is not enough.

I love seeing God rescue those who are cast down, broken-hearted, crushed and seemingly at the end, void of all hope.

I love seeing someone who has had so much pain, both physically and mentally, which would have destroyed so many, live in joy and freedom.

This is the miraculous story of Libby's life, transformed by the wonderful love and power of Jesus. This story takes us on a remarkable journey filled with truth and transparency along with outright honesty and vulnerability.

This story is Libby's heart crying out to those who are dealing with addictions, "There is hope".

Libby, my life has been made so much richer for knowing you. I am so grateful to God that He has given me such a wonderful spiritual daughter. I have been blessed and humbled by being able to reflect, although imperfectly, something of our Heavenly Father's heart towards you.

You have remained generous to others, through all your struggles. What an example you are!

Foreword

It wouldn't be right to finish this foreword without saying how I am so grateful for your husband Phil and two amazing children, Max and Gracie. What a beautiful family.

'The best is yet to come.'

Pastor Dave Shippam December 2024

To all who mourn in Israel,
   he will give a crown of beauty for ashes,
a joyous blessing instead of mourning,
   festive praise instead of despair.
In their righteousness, they will be like great oaks
   that the Lord has planted for his own glory.
Isaiah 61:3

Introduction

The fact that I have written this book is laughable. I have a story to tell, as I am sure you all do, but I am completely out of my depth in writing a book. Only in recent years have I begun to even read books. The largest credit for this belongs to my dear mother-in-law, Meryl. Her love for books is an inspiration and lit a small fire in me a few years ago, which grows every year. I have a hunger these days to learn and absorb information. I love to challenge and better myself. However, I have dyslexia, cannot spell or do maths and I struggle to read. It takes me a long time and I have only recently found it enjoyable. Also, I always thought that to write a book you need to be seen as successful in things, have loads of money, lots of followers and on the leadership team of a massive church. None of which applies to me but I, like everyone, am a work in progress and I hope this book will be a blessing to you.

2 Corinthians 12:9-10 says, *"'My grace is all you need. My power works best in weakness.' So now I am glad to boast about my weaknesses, so that the power of Christ can work through me. That's why I take pleasure in my weaknesses, and in the insults, hardships, persecutions, and troubles that I suffer for Christ. For when I am weak, then I am strong."*

In my daily life, when I share my testimony and life with people, often they say to me, "You should write a book!" However, it was not until December 2022 that I felt I received the green light from God to go ahead and do this.

When I talk about my life it always involves God because I have a relationship with Him and therefore will talk about Him a lot. Just as I do with my family. If you are

Introduction

in relationship with someone, of course you talk about them. They are a part of what makes you, you. So, for non-Christians reading this book, I'm aware that it is quite Bible-bashy. I will often refer to scripture, as I did above with the 2 Corinthians passage, but I encourage you to read the words and find what they mean to you.

Recently I decided to listen to the seven *Chronicles of Narnia* by CS Lewis on audiobook. I had built into my disciplines a 2-mile run most mornings, then collecting my little Pomeranian, taking him on a 2-mile walk. During that season of my life I would put on my headphones and get lost in a world of Narnia. Then I had breakfast with God, reading my Bible and journalling my thoughts and prayers.

God has used these Chronicles to talk to me and to inspire me in my every day walk with Jesus. Since I was a teenager, I have journalled and written down my prayers and thoughts in a notebook. I also spend time listening to God and writing down what I believe he is speaking into my heart. I believe the Holy Spirit started downloading spiritual insight relating to everyday life to me through my imagination from *The Chronicles of Narnia.*

I have found these inspirational and I want to share them with people. Therefore, throughout this book I will share some of these revelations as I share my life story with you, especially as they relate to my alcohol addiction and my journey to freedom.

At first, I was unsure about sharing my life story as I'm very aware it's not good to be obsessed with the past. Indeed, the Bible says, *"but I focus on this one thing: Forgetting the past and looking forward to what lies ahead,"* Philippians 3:13. However, the Bible also talks more about the word of our testimony and the power of remembering God's goodness and miraculous hand at work through the grace of our Lord Jesus. Billy Graham, a world-famous evangelist, said "The unbelieving world should see our testimony lived out daily because it just may point them to the Saviour." This is what I want to share with you; the goodness of God throughout my life and how He has always been there even when I was lost in addiction.

Psalm 22:22 says *"I will proclaim your name to my brothers and sisters. I will praise you among your assembled people."* Daniel 4:2 says *"I want you all to know about the miraculous signs and wonders the Most High God has performed for me."* Revelation 12:11 says, *"And they (the believers) have defeated him (the evil one – the devil) by the blood of the Lamb (Jesus's death) and by their testimony."*

My hope and prayer are that you will recognise God's mighty hand at work in your life, even if you don't have a relationship with Him yet, and you will realise that whatever you are going though right now, or have been through, God is a good, loving father. No matter what we have got ourselves caught up in, through choice or something that has been done to you, He is there for us. I encourage you to ask Him to reveal Himself afresh to you and let Him lovingly, gracefully and powerfully tend the soil of your heart.

My heart and prayer for us, together, through this book is that we will see our life as a garden and let God prune and tend to the gardens of our souls. Whatever is hidden in the darkness will be drawn to God's healing light. Let Him cut back what is overgrown and all that's running wild. Let all that has been planted, whether through pain or in joy, bear good fruit as we learn to surrender and abide in Jesus, the true Gardener. In John 15:5 Jesus says to His believers, *"Yes, I am the vine;*

Introduction

you are the branches. Those who remain in me, and I in them, will produce much fruit."

When I read or think about scripture, I have the John Legend song *All of me* in my head:

> *'Cause all of me*
> *Loves all of you*
> *Love your curves and all your edges*
> *All your perfect imperfections*
> *Give your all to me*
> *I'll give my all to you*
> *You're my end and my beginning*
> *Even when I lose, I'm winning*

God loves all of you, He not only loves you, He likes you! Give yourself to Him and He will give all of himself to you. Let Him, in His love, work on your imperfections. Then even when you are losing, when all seems to be going wrong around you, if you belong to Him, you will be anchored, and in Him, you will be winning.

Libby with her sister (left) and Mum on a happy day at the beach

Boots with a duck, just two of Libby's childhood pets

Dad in his traditional pose, cigarette in hand

Part One

My childhood

*"Remember the signs and believe the signs.
Nothing else matters."*

The Silver Chair, CS Lewis

1

My family

My childhood was not the best. I had a loving Christian mother who worked long hours as a nurse so we had enough money to get by. However, my father was an alcoholic who despised me the older I got, but loved my younger sister. He made no effort building any sort of relationship with me but seemed to enjoy my sister's company; he would listen to her, laugh with and cared for her, at least more than he did for me. However, he seemed to barely tolerate me and had very little interest in me. I have since spoken with a counsellor about this favouritism, who explained this may have been due to his dislike for himself due to his own upbringing and sense of self-worth. He hated himself and saw parts of himself in me and therefore hated me. Whether or not there is any truth in that idea, my childhood was what it was and unfortunately meant my own experience of our upbringing was a completely different story to my sister's, in certain parts of it.

My dad beat me, bullied me and disciplined me in ways that were completely out of control in the form of smacks, slippering and sometimes with a belt and a wooden spoon. On various occasions I received a solid punch to my face. Discipline was very different back in the 80s, but even by those standards the treatment I received from Dad was cruel and abusive. This is not to say I was the easiest child. My lack of respect for him and my disgust with his constant drunken behaviour led me to have a bad attitude and a sharp tongue towards him. However, I was still a child and most of those behaviours came as a result of his mistreatment of me.

My family

His behaviour, however ill or mentally disturbed he may have been, was completely unacceptable so I grew up with a lot of physical, emotional and mental damage. Of course, it was not all bad all of the time and my sister and I were the best of friends, and we had the most amazing imaginations. We would always make a game out of the very little we had, no matter where we were.

We would create and play imaginative games for hours and would quite often forget to eat as we were having so much fun together. We also had a lot of pets, which kept us busy and entertained. My dad loved animals, more than he loved me for sure, and would often come home from the pub with a new animal he had bought, rescued or traded for. I'm not even just talking about small animals like hamsters or rabbits. Dad would come home with farm animals like ducks and sheep, which would then live in our back garden. It made times even harder having so many extra mouths to feed, but unlike us, they never went hungry. I always found it strange that we had so many animals but we couldn't afford food, clothes and other normal things like wallpaper. We lived in a typical council house that had a roof, doors and windows but little else to give any of us much comfort.

The furniture we did have was handed down to us from my nanny. The electricity came through a coin-operated meter and would often turn off because we had no money to put in it. My sister and I used to find those evenings fun as we would light some candles and enjoy the whole thrill of doing everything by candlelight, which was good fun in our childish minds.

We lived on a street lined on both sides with council houses with a green in the middle, so there were lots of other children in the area. My sister and I had plenty of friends nearby, however even in those circumstances our family was still seen as the 'poor' one. Maybe it was our clothes or the smell of animals on us, but it did not stop us making friends. My sister is just over two years younger than me, so I always saw myself as her protector or bodyguard.

When I turned about ten, we were allowed to go into town by ourselves. We went into a little shop under the railway track that sold stationery. The shopkeeper was cold and stern looking, and she pointed out a sign on the door that said children were not allowed in her shop unattended by an adult. This made us really uncomfortable so we started to leave. As we walked out, my sister mumbled something under her breath that the woman must have heard. The next thing I knew, she and her adult son chased after us; she grabbed me and told us off. I can't remember what was said but I got slapped so hard across the face. It shocked me so much, and hurt, that we just turned around and ran home. My mum actually called the police when we told her about it, but when they came round to ask us about it, they told me off for causing trouble. I just took it and went to bed upset but I suppose I saw that as part of my role in protecting my sister.

My mum would work a lot, probably because my dad was in and out of work most of the time and would drink away what very little money we had. A few times when we were left in the care of my dad for the day, he would drive us to my nan's house and lock us in the garage for the whole day without even telling her. So, we entertained ourselves happily, playing with whatever we could find in there. I presumed he went and did a job for someone to get the cash to spend the rest of the afternoon in the pub. This was never a bother to me and my sister and never did I care. We would play and mess about with the G

My family

clamps and all the other tools and dangerous stuff in the garage. I remember twice my nan finding us after hearing strange noises coming from her garage and then calling round to the pubs to find my dad. This was before mobile phones so would have been a real hassle for her. She would call my mum up saying, "He's done it again!" as if it was my mum's fault, and that dad was blameless in this situation as he was working. I'm sure we were hungry and thirsty on these occasions as he didn't leave us with any food or drink, but I don't really remember because my sister and I had so much fun.

On other occasions, Dad would take us with him to the pub but not to treat us, just so he could get drunk while fulfilling his babysitting duties. He was always happiest when he was at the pub; to him it was like his real home amongst his real family. When getting dragged from pub to pub with Dad, he would just forget about us. My sister and I would often be so hungry, we played a game we called 'homeless people'. We would stealthily walk around the pub and eat the leftovers from people's plates, and drink the dregs from their glasses, around the pub and in the garden. It's so disgusting thinking about it now and who knows what we were drinking? There's no way on earth I would allow my children to do that. However, we had a great time even though looking back it is so gross.

2

Wanting Dad dead

As time went on, things got worse and worse between me and Dad. He got more violent towards me and seemed to hate me even more. I knew I was hard work at times, but I just didn't understand why my own dad despised me so much. It must have been really bad when I was about 10 years old, as I remember thinking of ways to kill Dad and then myself. I remember taking the bread knife from the kitchen on one occasion. Mum was working nights during this period, so I had plenty of time at home with just Dad and my sister. On this particular evening, I went further than just thinking about killing Dad – I actually stood over him with knife in hand as he slept in his drunken state in his bed. He was swearing and cursing at me or my mum in his sleep while I stood there for quite some time. I was thinking of where to stick the knife and then how I would be able to kill myself after. I wanted to die, but felt I could not leave my mum and sister to put up with Dad on their own. I'm not proud of it even now, but that was the only way I could comprehend putting an end to it all and protecting Mum and my sister.

Weirdly, the only thing that stopped me was the fact that someone had told me that suicide is a sin, and I might not go to heaven. It's strange that I didn't consider that murder is also a sin. I went to a Catholic school, so I think we had a lot of heavy teaching on sin. As a child I always thought God was disappointed or cross with me and it was impossible to please Him, so why bother? In this situation I honestly thought I was doing the world a favour if I killed Dad. It is so bad, but it shows how messed up and desperate I was in that moment and throughout my childhood. I often went to sleep in fear, for my mum's safety, mostly. I was constantly expecting a beating for something or other. It became my normal way of life. I was often woken by my mum in our room, having to pull out my under-bed mattress to sleep on because of Dad's drunken behaviour. He often lashed out and shouted obscenities in his sleep as well. I felt extremely vulnerable and deeply sad at bedtimes. This is probably why I am such a light sleeper nowadays. I can wake up even now to the slightest sound in or out of the house. This is so annoying as I wake up at least five times every night and then must try to fall asleep again, sometimes after investigating the noise first.

A few years ago, I remember waking up at about 3am because I heard a noise that sounded like stones bumping together. I looked out of the bedroom window and realised it was a neighbour's cat doing its business in our front garden. That's how super-sensitive I have become in my sleep. It's not a very useful skill, but maybe it will be one day if an assassin is sent to finish us off.

Around the time I was starting to fantasise about killing my dad, I remember starting to get involved in my mum and dad's arguments. I guess I was starting to get older, braver and was just getting fed up with Dad. Due to the alcohol and financial pressure they were under, they argued constantly. There was hardly a moment of peace. I wanted to defend Mum physically and emotionally. I got into so much trouble one day when I walked into the middle of one such fight, trying to protect my mum. I nearly got seriously hurt as I stood in front of my mum, but then she had to try to protect me when Dad turned on me instead.

Due to having dyslexia and ADHD (which I didn't discover until years later) and also the trauma of childhood abuse which impacted my school life, I didn't develop mentally or intellectually as well as most other children my age. I was distracted at school, slow to process information, struggled to read as I rarely practised at home and I fell behind the other children more and more every week. This affected me in many ways but two specific things I have struggled with over the years are processing things mentally and my memory. I recently realised I had muddled up some memories and merged them into one event. It is extremely frustrating, but I have been able to bring clarity to so many of my memories as I have been writing them down for this book and talking through them with my mum and sister.

Two such memories from these times became fused together in my brain but have now been separated. I created an image in my head of walking in on my mum getting attacked by Dad, who I thought was trying to kill her with a clothes iron. The reality though was quite surprising to me when I sat down and spoke to Mum about it.

The first incident involved the iron, which I always presumed in my head Dad was using as a weapon. As it turns out, my dad was trashing up the lounge in a fit of rage, trying to find money, whilst Mum was doing the ironing. It never ended well when Dad ran out of beer money and so he was taking it out on Mum. I walked in at the moment Mum had snapped and had enough. She had actually only just decided in her head that if he came near her in this moment she would fight back and attack Dad with the iron, but then had no need as I walked in and she assisted me out of the room – desperate times. My presence may actually have been useful for once.

The other time was when I walked in on Dad having thrown Mum into the chair. He was attacking her, so I went over to help my mum, which of course would have been no help as I was so young. Dad was throwing punches at her, but Mum had to take them as she was now holding me back, protecting me, as I tried to get him off her. Mum said after the ordeal was over, she stood up and realised not a single punch had hit her (the Lord's supernatural protection). My mum was cross with me for constantly getting involved, but it was out of love as she didn't want me to get hurt. I must have made it so much harder for her because she would have been trying to do the right thing, get control over a crazy situation and protect her child at the same time. I've never been able to walk past a bad situation without getting involved, much to the concern of my husband and children. Whether it be a person crying in the street, a seagull with a broken wing or a swan with fishing line stuck around its beak. I just can't walk by. This may come from my need and desire to be protected and even removed from countless awful situations as a child and not wanting anyone else, human or animal, to be left alone to get hurt. Dad would often come home in a bad mood and got annoyed at me for answering back or being cheeky. He got violent and chased me around the lounge, kicking me and throwing me around like a rag doll. I always wanted Mum to leave Dad for what he was doing to us, but she said she would only leave him if he was unfaithful to her, which didn't seem likely at the time as he was such a mess. My mum was aware of the emotional abuse, the neglect, the out of control 'discipline' and the hatred he had towards me, but has recently said she was unaware of the level of physical abuse that was going on. She had no external help and had to work a lot of hours to keep food on the table and a roof over our heads. In many ways she had three children to take care of on her own. I presumed Mum knew what was going on with Dad, right up to the writing of this book, but having spoken to her recently, she says she was unaware of the physical harm I was in and thought she had protected me. A lot of restoration and healing has come through discussion as a result of writing this book.

At other times I received beatings for not doing the housework to Dad's expectations. He was always very particular about dust and dog hair. That is ridiculous in itself, expecting a child to keep on top of the housework after school when her mum is at work, while most other children are doing their homework and out playing, having fun. This was my life though and to me it was normal, so I learnt that housework needs to be done thoroughly and not a speck of dirt left anywhere. Otherwise, I or the dog would pay the price. I also wanted to be a help to Mum and please her, so I didn't mind helping out. Even nowadays I do the vacuuming every day and can't rest if I know there is a mess somewhere in the house. I know I'm not going to get beaten if I don't clear it up, but there is something deeply ingrained in me that wants to do it.

Phil and the kids think I'm crazy and are always telling me to stop and chill out, but I think secretly they also like the fact that they don't have to do much of the housework.

3

Angel encounter

It wasn't long after the iron incident that my sister and I were snuggled up in bed together one night. There was an argument going on downstairs, which I was trying hard not to get involved in for once. Mum had told me not to and asked me to look after my sister. She and I would quite often get into bed and play games, like drawing on each other's backs and guessing what we were drawing. I used to stroke her hair to help her feel sleepy. I'm so grateful we had each other as it would have been even worse if I had been alone. Living through all these experiences brought us really close as well, although she doesn't remember all of the stories as she was so young at the time and she wasn't subject to the same abuse.

So, this particular night whilst Mum and Dad were having a full-on violent argument downstairs, we were distracting each other, playing these games. Neither one of us spoke about what was happening downstairs but I remember feeling scared for my mum, and I wanted to be downstairs protecting her. As we lay there staring up at the ceiling, we both got caught up in what I now know to be the same supernatural vision. As we looked up, the bed, my sister and I were the only physical things in the vision. The house was not there and around the bed was a host of enormous angels, fully human-looking apart from having massive white feathers like dazzling light-filled wings. They surrounded our bed and watched over us. My sister turned to me and said, "Isn't he beautiful?" I answered "Yes, he is. The black one?" She said "Yes." Out of this beautiful array of angels there was one with black skin; his face and amber eyes were breathtaking. My sister and I were in the same supernatural encounter seeing the same thing. All the angels were beautiful, but for whatever reason we both liked the black angel the best.

It still makes me cry to think of it now. A truly magical thing and something I have never forgotten. In our childlike minds it seemed normal that we both saw this. We didn't really talk about it as if it was spectacular, just as if it was the norm. We then slept a deep and peaceful sleep.

My sister lost her faith in God during her teenage years and is not a believer now. I am working on it, and more importantly, so is God. However, I recently asked if she remembered the angel vision, and she said she did and that it gave her shivers to think of it. She remembers us seeing the same vision and remembers the black angel standing out from all the rest. It's like the story of Peter Pan; we forget the magic and wonders that happen to us in our childhood years when we become adults. We usually put it down to having a childish imagination. I wonder how many times we have forgotten things like this because we don't talk about them and choose not to remember through fear of looking weird or different. It came as such a relief to me that she could remember. Angels are sent to those who will receive salvation, as I believe and want for my sister.

I feel as though the older I got the more messed up I became. I loved Jesus, but because of my home life being so vulnerable and chaotic, I was also quite fearful. Not of pain or Dad hurting me, as this was normal, but I was so very fearful of my mum dying. She was my world and I thought that if she died, how would I care for my sister? Would we become slaves to Dad and his alcoholic lifestyle? It was about the age of 10 that I started to hear voices in my head. I now believe this was demonic but as a child

Angel encounter

that was already messed up, I listened to them and saw them as another part of me. The voices would tell me I had to do things and if I did not do them then Mum would die! The voices would tell me to brush my teeth ten times or put all my teddies into bed or step only on certain steps walking up the stairs. It was exhausting but in my fragile mind I needed to obey.

I did eventually tell Mum about these thoughts, and she taught me the thoughts were the devil lying to me to make me live in fear and be controlled by him. My pastor uses the acronym that the word FEAR broken down is False Expectation Appearing Real. My mum taught me the devil or the demonic powers are terrified of Jesus. There is power in the name of Jesus. She taught me when I had these thoughts I needed to say (out loud if I could), "In the name of Jesus, be gone." I started to do this, and still do today, and it always works. The bad thoughts go from my mind when I ask Jesus for help. I encourage you next time you hear negative voices in your head to say out loud if you dare, "In the name of Jesus, be gone." When you are struggling with voices in your head that you know are not normal or thoughts that are not healthy, don't accept them. We can't do everything in our own strength. Overcome them in the name of Jesus.

4

Hitchhiking

Another angel story I like to tell happened a few years later. One evening, I was on my way to a youth church meeting at St James' Church in Coventry with my best friend. We had never taken the bus into Coventry before, and we accidentally got off way too early and found ourselves lost. I now know where we were, and we really weren't that lost, but at the time we didn't have a clue and were a bit freaked out.

Anyway, in our naivety and stupidity we started talking about what we should do. These were the days before mobile phones, and we couldn't see a pay phone anywhere. I'm pretty sure it was my friend's suggestion, but her idea was to hitchhike! I had never done anything like this before and was not too keen on the idea. I was about 14 and she is nearly three years older than me. We talked about the fact that maybe this would not be safe, so we prayed that God would send us a white car to prove to us this would be a safe option. Crazy right?! This was also before Ubers and besides, we didn't have the money for a taxi anyway.

So, we carried on walking, heading in the direction we thought we should be going, looking out for the white car we hoped God would send us. All of a sudden, from nowhere appeared a little old lady who was out jogging. She had white hair, with a white dog and she was wearing a white cagoule. She jogged up to us and asked how she could help. We explained we were lost and trying to find St James' Church. She said, "Girls follow me, you will have to jog but I will show you the way."

Hitchhiking

So, we jogged behind this lovely old lady, giggling about the fact she was in white, and this must be an answer to prayer. She stopped after a while and pointed us the rest of the way. She told us to go straight ahead at the bottom of the road and then on the left we would find the church. We could see where she was talking about and when we both turned to say thank you, she had completely vanished. There really wasn't anywhere she could have gone in such a short time. It reminds me of a great verse from the book of Hebrews that says, *"Therefore, angels are only servants—spirits sent to care for people who will inherit salvation."* Hebrews 1:14. She was clearly an angel, so cool.

It makes me wonder how many other times in my life I have seen angels but not even realised they were there.

5

Mum goes away

In Year 10, when I was 14 and in my first year of GCSEs, my chaotic home life came to a head as my mum decided to go on holiday to see friends in America and leave me and my sister with Dad at home. Bad idea. My sister was excited to stay with friends, but I didn't want to because I felt it was my responsibility to take care of the animals. I couldn't trust my dad to look after and feed them. At this time, we owned a dog and a cat. My dog was a Border Collie called Boots because she was black but with white feet that looked as if she had boots on. She was such a lovely dog, full of unconditional love and was a real Godsend to me, especially when things got really bad with Dad, because she was so loyal and would always stay by my side. I would cuddle her, which always gave me a sense that I was loved and needed. My cat was black and white, absolutely massive and called William, named after a boy that my sister and I knew. He was the size of a dog and had the attitude to match.

We also had lots of other random animals at different times in our lives as Dad brought them home from the pub. We had a sheep, a ferret, a goat, ducks, quails, guinea pigs, rabbits, gerbils, hamsters, stick insects and goldfish as well as a pig, which fortunately never actually came to our house.

Dad would have completely forgotten about the dog and cat if I hadn't been around. On a few occasions, when he was in a drunken state, he left the dog tied up on the street by the corner shop and forgot to bring her home. He would then fall asleep leaving Mum and me to go off searching the streets to find the shop or pub where he had left her. Several times we would find her still tied to a lamppost, sitting there with her ears up waiting to be collected. Such a good girl.

Despite being an animal-lover, my dad often used the animals to hurt me. On one horrendous occasion as a punishment to me for not cleaning the dog hair off the carpets, he decided to cut off Boots' hair. That would be bad enough but he was drunk and used wallpaper scissors! All just to teach me a lesson. The outcome was horrific. It was not a pretty sight to say the least and it is the most traumatic memory I have. I can bear the pain I went through, but to think of one of the animals suffering really hurts me, which is exactly why my dad did it. On this occasion, I came home from primary school on my own, as my sister went to her friend's house for tea. I remember being sad all day at school because of something Dad had been moaning about before school. Anyway, I walked in the front door and noticed dog hair in big chunks on the carpet followed by drops of blood. Dreading what I might find, I followed the trail all the way to the back door where my poor Boots was curled up; sad and hurting. She didn't stand to welcome me as she usually did. Dad was in a drunken sleep in his armchair and next to him were the wallpaper scissors. Poor Boots probably did nothing to protect herself and just let Dad hack her hair off. She had cuts and scratches all over her. It was so sad.

As a result, I couldn't take her for a walk in public for a good month or so, as she would have been taken away from us by animal rescue. With hindsight this would have been better for her. I know that now, but in my childlike brain I thought she needed me. In truth, it was I who needed her; she was my friend and ally. She knew how badly we both were treated and she stayed with me through it all.

My mum nursed her wounds with disinfectant. She looked such a state, poor dog. I feel sadder about the mistreatment of my dog, than about what I have been through. Dad often had crazy outbursts of anger and I think when he had been drinking he would beat Boots for getting in the way or something. I know he beat her when she was heavily pregnant because I remember thinking it was his fault one of her puppies was stillborn. It's the behaviour of a true monster to beat animals and children.

As for William, the cat – my dad decided all cats were evil, apart from my nanny's cat. So, he didn't give him the time of day and would never have fed him if I was away. Anyway, going back to my mum's holiday to America; she had been invited out there alone, so we were left behind at home. I decided I needed to stay at home as I felt it was my duty to look after the animals. From a very young age I felt the protector of my mum, sister and all our animals. I grew up quickly with this overwhelming sense of responsibility. This was useful in some ways, but it meant I missed out on the simplicity of just being a child and having fun with the security of two loving parents.

Fortunately, my sister went to stay at her friend's house while my mum was away so she wasn't there to witness the worst and final physical encounter I had with our dad.

6

The final beating

Before leaving me alone for two weeks, my mum put me in charge of the house. I was already in charge of the housework and cooking dinner by this point as Dad was incapable of looking after himself properly, let alone a wife and two daughters. So, Mum told me what I needed to do and gave me enough cash to pay for the food, electricity meter and anything else that needed paying for during the next fortnight. In my young and naïve mind, I thought this was great as I was finally the person officially in charge around the house but I didn't fully consider how it might affect my already poor relationship with Dad.

One afternoon, after my mum had left, my dad came home very drunk and started to bully, poke and push me around. He had worked out Mum had given me all the money and he wanted it. Things got out of hand, and I said some things I shouldn't. Dad, in his extreme anger and frustration in wanting some money to go to the pub, attacked me, throwing punches at me. He full-on punched me in the face; I fell to the floor. In hatred and anger towards me he bent down shouting in my face to get out of the house and never come home, and if I did, he would kill me. I believed him and before I could even pack a bag I ran out and went to go and stay with my best friend and her wonderful mum and dad in Kenilworth.

I was always concerned back then that if anyone found out about the abuse, I would get taken away and never see my mum or sister again.

The school found out this time as I had a bruised cheek and when I fled from my house, I left without my school uniform or any of my books or equipment. I can honestly say I just assumed everybody else's dads were the same, so I didn't really feel it was a big deal. We had no social media back then, so there was nothing to compare my life to. No one said anything to me about Dad's behaviour apart from the odd comment here and there, usually in joke rather than concern. Dad had even beaten me in front of a primary school friend one day. He picked me up and threw me across the floor. I was totally humiliated and embarrassed, so I just walked away. I don't remember her saying anything to me afterwards. She never came round again after this, funnily enough, and didn't hang out with me much at school either.

7

Did people know?

One of my favourite quotes is, "All it takes for evil to prevail in this world is for good people to do nothing". This has profound relevance to me and my upbringing as I look back and wonder how different it could have been if someone had done something to help me, and ultimately rescue me, by taking me out of our house.

When I was 18 years old, I found out my grandmother knew what I had gone through and had wanted to do something about it. She expressed extreme remorse to me and regretted not pushing harder to help me. She said at one time she had brought it up with me in conversation but I got defensive towards my dad and was angry and emotional. So, she decided to drop it. It was one of those situations where it was alright for me to talk badly about my dad and even hate him, but it was not OK for anyone else to! He was my dad after all, and I loved him as well as hated him. It is definitely a real but confusing thing to love and hate someone at the same time.

In those early adult years, my grandma and I talked a lot about Dad and how messed up my upbringing was. I actually found it comforting and validating that I wasn't over-exaggerating or making a deal out of nothing. She said she wished she had pushed harder to get me out of the house or got Mum to make him leave. It's hard because this was never discussed in front of my mum; it was like the elephant in the room situation.

Despite the fact I was not rescued from my dad, there was one person I will always remember with fondness, who really made a difference in my life. I had the most amazing teacher in Year 6 at my primary school who I believe knew things weren't right at home for me. She took me under her wing and loved me a lot. She tried to encourage me in my learning and would question me about my home life a lot. Don't forget in the early 90s it was legal and generally accepted to smack your children. I remember her questioning me about some marks I had on my bum once when I was changing for PE and I told her I was smacked for wasting electricity. This was what Dad had told me I was doing. In fact, I was under the dining table vacuuming the dog hair out of the corners, which he had told me to do. However, I was obviously taking too long doing it in his opinion. Therefore, he dragged me out from under the table and beat me up for it. Anyway, after she questioned me, nothing happened, no one saved me, and actually even if someone had reported it to Social Services I would never have wanted to be taken away. I wanted to stay at home because I loved my mum and sister so much. I can see why children in care run away, it's hard when all you have known is disfunction. You learn to live with it as it is your normal way of life.

Our neighbours had obviously noticed and heard things in the house. A few comments were made to my mum and concern for her welfare was expressed, but no one thought I or my sister were in danger.

I also remember neighbours coming round one night to inform us Dad had passed out around the corner by the garages and was lying on the ground in a bloody mess. I and my sister were home alone and so we went to get him. I actually remember us thinking it was quite funny taking an arm and a leg each and trying to carry him but then we took a leg each and just dragged him back home, leaving him in the hallway of our house. We even pulled him up a few concrete steps. Ouch!

Did people know?

On the occasion when Mum was away, I was 15, nearly 16 and honestly did not want to be taken to live away from my mum, sister and the animals. Despite the offer from my year head and a woman from Social Services to find me foster care, I refused. I was older and wiser and thought I could handle Dad. As far as I was aware, school, Social Services and my best friend's mum had agreed I would stay with her until my mum came home. I was told a safeguarding officer had been sent round to my house and had told my dad off and he had been warned about his outbursts and recommended anger management. I remember this being a comfort to me that someone had gone to the house and had a firm word with him, however my mum can't remember this, probably because she was in America, and I have no way of ever knowing if these things actually happened.

Like most bullies, my dad was just a scared little boy really, so a warning with a threat would have helped. I remember Mum coming home from her time away. I wanted to go home and see my sister and animals but was fearful of Dad. I had never been fearful of him before this occasion. I was so consumed with anger and hatred towards him, I never noticed the feeling of being scared. Obviously, I felt the pain of being physically hurt by him, but somehow it was just the norm and fear was not something I had. For some reason I was more fearful of my mum, sister and dog being physically hurt and would have stepped in the way without a thought to myself at all – even if it meant dying for them. However, this time I was scared to go home and I just wanted to live with my best friend and her parents forever. I had a lovely relationship with her dad, and it felt so good to be liked and loved by him. My mum encouraged me to come home despite all the trouble that had occurred and I don't remember ever talking to my dad again after my return home until I became an adult.

We both just pretended the other one didn't exist and he never talked to me about the situation. He never said sorry or showed any remorse. It's hard living like that, but it's what makes me think someone in authority had been and had a stern word. It worked, if indeed they did.

Little by little, rejection, anger, hatred and disgust became the garden of my soul. It is strange to think like this but I no longer had any relationship with my dad. He gave me no attention at all, which may sound like a good thing as before this the attention was mostly negative, but at least it was something. Children need and crave attention from their parents and all of a sudden, I wasn't getting any from my dad, despite living in the same house. It was a new level of rejection I had to come to terms with. I cried a lot and when asked what was wrong by my mum, I would never know how to answer as I didn't fully understand what was going on. One day my sister asked me once why I cried all the time and I full-on beat her up with a hairbrush because I was so angry inside. Not to mention confused by the whole situation. I was severely punished by Dad for this. He took the opportunity to revisit old behaviours and saw it as a valid excuse, I think, to beat me for hurting my sister.

I know that was a bad one that day as I remember wetting myself as I tried to run from him. Despite everything going on in the house as well as in my head, I was getting closer and closer to God. I prayed every night. I gave all my feelings and pain to God. I knew He was real and I knew He loved me from a very young age. I loved Him and still do.

8

Prayer

My prayers weren't always healthy. I prayed every night religiously, "Please God, kill my dad or make him a Christian." This was my ritual prayer. I had accepted I wasn't allowed to kill him myself, but hoped God might do it for me. I actually believe God answered my childhood prayers in one swoop and I will tell you about this later.

Despite my constant pleading with my mum to kick Dad out or even leave him and take us with her, she stayed with Dad in the hope he would become a Christian. Since I have become an adult, my mum has said Dad threatened to take my sister and me away from her if she ever left or made him leave. Unfortunately, she believed him and she also always desired that God would make Dad change. She hoped Dad would become a Christian, which she believed would solve everything.

Just a side note here, never marry a man or woman in the hope they change. It will be damaging to you and your children at a later stage. Nothing short of a miracle can change a person from years of living life their way.

Anyway, this is my story to tell, not my mum's, and I don't want to blur the lines. She had her own horrors to deal with and has her own story to tell, if she chooses. It was a different time we were living in, in the 90s. Nowhere near as much help and support for breaking away from abusive situations as we have access to now. Only extreme violence was seen as abuse as smacking was legal, which caused confusion for the out-of-control discipline that took place in some places. The laws and help were not easily accessed. This lifestyle could be considered the norm and the vulnerable tolerated it. My mum has stated she was unaware of the level of physical abuse I suffered, as it all happened when she was out. She is truly sorry for not have taking me and my sister out of the situation sooner. She said she thought she could stop being my dad's wife but there would be no way she could stop him from being our father. I will continue with my own story.

Prayer became a massive part of my life. It kept me in touch with God, whom I realised loved me more than any human being could. No matter what my dad did to me, he couldn't stop me praying and could not separate me from God's love. Praying to God brought me a measure of peace and joy even in the midst of some awful circumstances and I still spend time in prayer with God every day. In the good times and bad, God is there as my rock and my fortress. I also spend time reading the Bible and listening to Him to receive His word for my life and family. I always struggled with reading and so I didn't enjoy it – I found it hard work. As I mentioned earlier, my mother-in-law inspired me to take up reading more recently. She is way ahead of me, having bookshelves filled with books new and old, numbering over a thousand. I don't have books on display, so when I finish one, I pass it on to someone else who I think may enjoy it.

Now when I read, especially the Bible, I am catching up on so many years where I didn't read and so I am desperate to find meaning in every word.

9

Dad leaves – hooray!

Life ticked on OK for a while. My dad never laid a finger on me again, but I still wanted him gone. He was unrepentant and caused a horrible atmosphere at home. Then one day everything changed, when I received some new information. I can't remember how I found this out, but I had heard that my dad was spending a lot of time at a lady's house in Whitnash. For whatever reason I followed him and realised he was having an affair. I don't know the exact details of this, but he stayed the night with this lady a lot. This was great news for me, which I loved. Firstly, he was out of the way so I could live in peace at home and secondly, it was the answer I had been praying for.

I was delighted for my mum as well because I knew this gave her a way out, biblically speaking. She had told me God doesn't like divorce and the only two ways she could be free of Dad would be through death or if he committed adultery. Anyway, once I was sure about what Dad was getting up to, I was so happy telling Mum. I didn't have a care in the world for how she would feel about this, which with hindsight I feel bad about, but it was such a weight off my shoulders. I'm not even sure now how it impacted her. Again, I have cut details where I don't know them as I need the story to be mine, but also accurate.

My dad didn't want to leave initially, probably because he had it easy at home with meals on the table and everyone else tidying up around him. He was also living off Mum's wage most of the time, except when he got odd jobs here and there. However, now Mum had decided she wanted him gone, it was inevitable. Dad finally decided to pack his bags and leave one day when I was out at work. I worked for a Council-run babysitting scheme, so was off across town somewhere looking after someone else's children and no doubt their pets as well. I loved this job because I loved little children and animals, but I also thrived on the sense of responsibility. Usually, the parents were really grateful as well, which was a nice experience for me.

So, on one such day, my mum and I sat down and wrote a letter on paper to leave for Dad (which is what we used to do before phones, email and the internet). We then went off to work, unsure of what we might face when we got home that evening. I remember coming home almost nervous about what might greet me, but I was delighted to see there was no sign of Dad. He had packed all his old junk into a bag and got out of the house, never to return again. I don't know how it happened or if there was any trouble, because my over-riding emotions were happiness and relief that he was finally gone.

I came into the house, had a quick look around to see whether he had left or not and then I celebrated as only I know how to. I cleaned the house. Not very exciting, I know but it was a fresh start for me and I wanted to remove every trace of my dad. I also wanted to make it nice and girly for my mum, my sister and me to enjoy from now on. When my mum came home, she also was relieved and happy, but the reality hit her later that night and she spent most of the evening crying.

I was pleased for my mum and sister of course, but on a personal level, having been subjected to abuse over so many years from my dad, I just felt so happy and free. I imagined my life would be so easy from now on, now there was no more Dad. But of course, this was not true.

10

The assault

I'm now 17 years old and I'm studying a Level 3 Diploma at a college in Leamington Spa, Warwickshire. Back in school, my GCSE exam results weren't the best, but I couldn't have done any more than I did in preparation. As well as having a disturbed home life, I was also dyslexic and had ADHD (not particularly hyperactive, but with an inability to concentrate and retain information), which wasn't the most suitable recipe for achieving As and Bs in Year 11. When we had mock exams, Mum and I quickly realised I was likely to fail everything, so Mum encouraged me to focus on one subject we thought I could possibly pass. We decided on drama because I really enjoyed it and I was quite good at it. My mum spent lots of time with me reading through *The Crucible* and helping me to learn and almost memorise the text for my written paper in drama. In the end, I was actually delighted to get an A in drama and a C in art. I have always been a creative person and I found these subjects easier to understand.

I then went to college and spent a year studying Health and Social Care Level 2 so I could move on to Level 3 the following year, as I didn't have enough GCSEs to go straight on to the course. I got a Merit in Level 2, which meant I could do an A-level subject or equivalent in the September. Things were finally looking up.

A few years after our children were born, I decided I wanted to join the police. I looked into the entry requirements and realised I needed at least a grade C in English and Maths GCSE. I was already working at the time, so I decided to go back to college in the evenings and try to get the English qualification first. I chose English Literature because that seemed a bit easier for me to get my head round. I attended every week for around 9 months and managed to get a C grade, which I was delighted about. Then I took on Maths, which has always been so hard for me to understand. I started at college again but very soon realised I just couldn't understand even the basics. So regretfully, I gave up on my dream to join the police and the maths course.

Anyway, back to college at the age of 16 and I was approaching the end of my one-year Level 2 course. I really wanted to be a nurse at this point as everyone else in my family seemed to be nurses. During these years I became involved in a Christian youth group called the Pulse, which met in Coventry at about 7pm. My friend Beth and I used to get a bus home from the group at about 10pm. It dropped us in town, which was about a 20-minute walk from my house. One evening, after we had been to Pulse, we were walking home, down Brunswick Street and we walked past a side alley where they used to have a market, probably still do. There was a group of teens about my age up to no good and smoking weed – three boys and one girl. The girl was clearly the leader; she had an intimidating presence and was all dressed in gothic clothing, not to mention clearly high.

I thought nothing of it and was not intimidated by this, so carried on walking. The council estate I was brought up on constantly had issues with youths behaving anti-socially, getting up to mischief, fighting and falling out. A lot of angry, messed up, poverty-stricken families like my own all squeezed into a small over-populated area. This was the norm.

Anyway, walking home chatting and laughing with Beth, it soon became clear this group was following us.

The assault

They stepped out of the dark alley and shouted, "Are you Diane f***ing Rofe?" (I changed my name by deed-poll to Libby, short for Elizabeth, which runs in the family. I hated the name Diane as it has no special meaning and my dad chose it for me because he fancied a barmaid with the same name.) We tried to walk away and Beth wanted to knock on a door to ask for help, but I assured her it will be fine. In fact, I said to her that we didn't need to worry as "God was with us". They carried on following us while laughing and intimidating us. They kept asking if I was Diane or not. I recognised the girl and knew she was the daughter of the woman my alcoholic dad was seeing and now, presumably, living with. I knew this girl from my primary school. She was in the year below me and was a bully back then. I turned to answer her but she got right in my face and said my dad had told her mum that I had said her mum was a "fat cow." I don't think I had said this, but couldn't swear to it. I tried to assure this girl and her bully followers I was glad Dad was out of my life and I didn't have to worry about his actions any longer. Little did I know I was in the middle of another one of the consequences of his drunken life. They seemed to follow me around, even when I thought I was free.

    She wasn't interested in anything I had to say and so she grabbed me and said, "If I hear it again I will f***ing kill you!" I thought to myself, "You won't hear it again," but I kept quiet. Both Beth and I were scared. We were both quite small and certainly no match for a bully and three boys. They continued to follow us all the way down Brunswick Street. They were mocking, heckling and spurring one another on, trying to get a response from me. Before I knew it, a nasty painful yank to my hair pulled me straight to the ground. I hit my head on the pavement with such a bang I think I was slightly concussed. Coming round the front of me she said, "I heard it again." She lifted me like I weighed nothing, by the clothes on my chest. The boys grabbed Beth and covered her mouth. I wanted to cry out, but no sound came from my mouth! It was just like in a nightmare where you have no voice. I was silenced by fear and also dizziness from my head wound. She said, "I heard it again, so I am going to kill you." She repeatedly punched me in the face, countless times; I wanted to die. The pain was so bad. She threw me to the floor, then smashed my face into a low wall. She then kicked me all over my body and spat in my beaten-up face. When she got bored, she took over holding Beth and commanded each of the boys to kick me. I was barely conscious by the time they left.

My face swelled up so quickly, I thought I was blind. Beth helped me to my feet and somehow, we made it home. She called 999 from the landline. This was before the times of mobile phones so we had to wait until we got home. We had a phone on the wall with a curly wire. The medic on the end of the phone was trying to keep me awake as I just wanted to give in and sleep. The ambulance arrived at the same time my mum came home. I don't remember too much after that apart from the concern on my mum's face and of course the pain. The pain was so bad, there was not a part of my head I could lie on that wasn't bruised or sore.

The months following the attack were unpleasant as well, because the girl was threatening and intimidating me to make me pull out of taking her to court. A long story short, as far as I'm aware she went to a Young Offenders Institution for three months. I don't think the boys were held to account at all. Not a very impressive sentence for such a violent attack.

The assault

The newspaper article said the girl: "punched and kicked a former friend to the ground and then spat in her face." What a joke. We had never been friends. The newspaper also made a deal about my knee, probably because of the amount of blood, but my knee was the least of my concerns. It was my face that was the problem.

The attack was the straw that broke the camel's back. I felt I had a target on my head and a sign on my back saying: "Beat me and treat me badly" as I had been mistreated by so many people. As well as Dad hitting me, I was also hit by a special needs teaching assistant who was assigned to me. She got frustrated by my low learning ability and slapped me across the face when I couldn't answer a question. A fellow pupil ran to get help and we never saw the teaching assistant again. I've also been punched by a random stranger and, as shared previously, been hit by the shopkeeper's son.

Just when I thought I was free from Dad, his lifestyle choices meant I had been attacked again. It seemed to follow me around. I was a bit of a wreck, with a bruised body and a messed-up face. I quit college, though I was in the middle of a two-year Level 3 diploma. I was actually at the top of the class for the first time in my life and doing well, but the assault took my confidence away.

Over the next few months, I was angry, scared, lost and broken. I worked in a nursing home part time so I still had that to focus on, but I also spent a lot of time at church and doing church things. I was involved in every church activity, home groups, prayer meetings – whatever was happening – I went along. Just before the assault I had told my friend that God was with us. I still believe it now, even though at the time I thought that meant we would not get physically hurt. God has always been right there with me, through the highs and the lows.

Christmas Day, 11-year-old Libby cooked dinner while her mum was working as a nurse

Girl kicked and spat at old friend

A WHITNASH teenager punched and kicked a former friend to the ground and then spat in her face, a court has heard.

The 16-year-old, who cannot be named for legal reasons, pounced on her teenage victim as she walked along Clemens Street in Leamington, Mid-Warwickshire Youth Court was told.

The victim was pulled by the hair, punched in the face and then kicked while she lay on the pavement, magistrates heard yesterday. Her assailant then spat in her face before running away from the 11pm incident.

The victim suffered extensive bruising and swelling to her face and right knee and needed hospital treatment.

In mitigation, the court heard the assailant believed the victim had insulted her mother and that a recent meeting between the former school friends had passed without incident.

Magistrates ordered the teenager, who pleaded guilty to actual bodily harm, to be put on probation for a year.

The story reached the local newspaper, though the attacker was never Libby's friend

With her friend a few weeks after the assault, Libby's black eye is still visible

Part Two

New beginnings

*"'But of course,' he thought, 'I was quite safe.
That is why the Lion kept on my left.
He was between me and the edge all the time."*
The Horse and His Boy, CS Lewis

11

The Lord makes a way

From this point on, things started to get better for me. Despite being badly bruised and on the verge of dropping out of college, my life started heading on a new path. God was still leading and directing me along the way, but the abuse was behind me and I was walking into a new chapter in my life. Of course, the effects of the abuse were still with me and in some ways have made me who I am today, but over the years God has healed wounds. Even now He uses those early, horrible experiences in life to help me be a comfort to other people who are going through similar things.

One amazing story, which I must tell you about, was that during this time, after my assault, I wanted to get out of our council estate. I spent all my time in Kenilworth, as this is where the church was and my pastor and his family, my job at the care home and my best friend and her family. My mum also wanted a move as she was looking for a fresh start. We both love Kenilworth. My sister wasn't too fussed but was excited to move and also had friends in Kenilworth. At the time my pastor was teaching on, *"The earnest prayer of a righteous person has great power and produces wonderful results"* from James 5:16. (My pastor back then, by the way, is still my pastor and spiritual father now, our best friends. We assist him in the leading of the church I have been planted in since I was 14 years old – over 28 years).

I remember my mum sat me and my sister down and we prayed as fervently as we could that we would get a council house exchange into Kenilworth. My mum rang the Council, and they pretty much laughed her off the phone. We were told we would be on a three-year waiting list, despite my mum explaining the assault and the state of my mental health living on the estate. Anyway, my mum said not to be disheartened and we prayed and proclaimed we would live in Kenilworth. Days later – yes, days – we got a call from the Council saying, "this has never happened before, but a family from Warwick wants to move into Leamington, an elderly couple in Kenilworth wants to move to Warwick and you want to move from Leamington to Kenilworth. Would you be willing to do a three-way swap? All of them are three bedrooms, one bathroom council housing, no viewing, just an agreement." Mum asked, "Where is the house in Kenilworth?" The lady said, "Albion Street". God had not only provided the house and the way, but the house was on the same street as the church. Thank you, Lord.

We were delighted as this was my first experience of answered prayer, although I'm sure there were many more before that I didn't realise or appreciate. Now I was filled with faith, confidence, encouragement and a sense I had God on my side. Romans 8:31 says *"If God is for us, who can ever be against us?"* I had a realisation and hope He had a plan for my life and He saw and heard me. Psalm 139:17 says *"How precious are your thoughts about me, O God. They cannot be numbered!"* We moved very quickly after this. The whole church helped as there was a lot of work to do on the new house. Even a few young people from a small youth group I helped to lead. It was a crazy but wonderful time.

12

New beginnings

During the summer of 1999, when I was halfway through my two-year diploma, we went to Faith Camp, a Christian camp run by the church where my pastor and his wife did their ministry training. Kingdom Faith Church in Horsham was led by the late Pastor Colin Urquhart, who was a wonderful man of God and spiritual father to my pastor. We had been to Faith Camp once before and had loved it. The youth work was great and we always made new friends.

This time, during the meeting one evening I felt a burning in my heart to go to Bible School. To do this would mean giving up the dream to be a nurse and instead choose to live a life surrendered to God. Part of me wanted this, but the stronger part wanted to work hard, earn money and be successful. I felt like going to Bible School would be signing up to be a poor and super-spiritual nut job for the rest of my life. Also, going to Bible College cost a lot of money, which we did not have. I ignored the feeling and didn't tell anyone.

At the youth service the following night a leader was talking on stage and he stopped, pointed to me in front of everyone and said, "If you do not obey God and His calling, you will grieve this for the rest of your life." Weird thing to say! But it totally got my attention, and was exactly what I needed to hear. However, I still ignored it, the camp ended and we came home.

September was fast approaching, and I was down in the dumps, unsure what to do and still messed up from all the abuse I had suffered. My mum sat me down and said, "What is God telling you to do? Because I know what

New beginnings

He is saying to me, and I'm waiting to hear you say it." I told her about the word and the desire to give up on my course and to go to Bible School, but also the fears. We went to see our pastor. He was in full support of it and made a few calls. As well as attending the college as a student himself a few years previously, he also went on to work there so he knew a lot of the staff who still worked there. Although I missed the sign-up date, he got me in to Bible College and the church put in the money to send me there. (Thank you, my lovely church family, for your investment in my life.) So, I chose to obey God rather than follow my own desires and I'm so glad I did.

13

Bible College

Bible School was hard for me at first; weird yet wonderful. I can honestly say, looking back, they were the best and most life-changing two years of my life. Despite the fact I had decided to just go there to meet with God and fall more in love with God and not with a man, I fell in love, deep and hard, with Phil. He was (and is still) amazing and a key part in my healing journey. I actually didn't realise I had a story to tell, until I met him. He helped me heal by making me realise my childhood was not normal or safe. Neither was it acceptable how I had been treated. A lot of forgiveness was needed to my mum more than my dad, as he was the one who was ill, and she was the Christian in all of it.

Forgiveness is a choice and even now telling you this story I choose to forgive. However, I really don't feel any unforgiveness nowadays. I'm very aware that what the devil intended for evil, God has made good. As it says in Genesis 50:20, *"You intended to harm me, but God intended it all for good. He brought me to this position so I could save the lives of many people."*

I'm very pleased I have been through trials and the older I get, the more I learn that any trial can destroy you and make you a victim, or it can make you a warrior and a victor. I love the fact that every time something comes against me, it draws me closer to God. In John 16:33 Jesus says, *"I have told you all this so that you may have peace in me. Here on earth you will have many trials and sorrows. But take heart, because I have overcome the world."*

Bible College

There are many things I could say here, but it is important I tell my story not my mum's or anyone else's. The following extract is from *The Horse and His Boy* in the Narnia series from CS Lewis I love so much. As well as showing the need to stick to my own story, it also speaks of how God is with us always, even when we don't realise. It is a conversation between Aslan the lion (Large Voice), who represents God, and a boy called Shasta who has just experienced a few things that he didn't like or understand.

"Oh, I am the unluckiest person in the whole world?"
...
"I do not call you unfortunate," said the Large Voice.
"Don't you think it was bad luck to meet so many lions?" said Shasta. "There was only one lion," said the Voice.
"What on earth do you mean? I've just told you there were at least two the first night, and——"
"There was only one: but he was swift of foot."
"How do you know?"
"I was the lion." And as Shasta gaped with open mouth and said nothing, the Voice continued. "I was the lion who forced you to join with Aravis. I was the cat who comforted you among the houses of the dead. I was the lion who drove the jackals from you while you slept. I was the lion who gave the Horses the new strength of fear for the last mile so that you should reach King Lune in time. And I was the lion you do not remember who pushed the boat in which you lay, a child near death, so that it came to shore where a man sat, wakeful at midnight, to receive you."
"Then it was you who wounded Aravis?"
"It was I."
"But what for?"

"Child," said the Voice, "I am telling you your story, not hers. I tell no-one any story but his own."

"Who are you?" asked Shasta.

"Myself," said the Voice, very deep and low so that the earth shook: and again "Myself," loud and clear and gay: and then the third time "Myself," whispered so softly you could hardly hear it, and yet it seemed to come from all round you as if the leaves rustled with it.

Shasta was no longer afraid that the Voice belonged to something that would eat him, nor that it was the voice of a ghost. But a new and different sort of trembling came over him. Yet he felt glad too.

Shasta was annoyed that his friend Aravis got hurt at the hand of Aslan. But as hard as this is to understand, this was to be a part of the bigger picture. I love the way Aslan says, "I am telling you your story, not hers. No one is told any story but their own." I often think this through when I'm defending myself for the things I do wrong, when I blame circumstances, my upbringing, my dad for the abuse, my mum for seemingly doing nothing to save me from it or even God for allowing it. Or like Shasta, just feeling the unluckiest person in whole world. Some people will blame the police, the law, Social Services, school or even Christians and the church. The list can go on and on. But at the end of the day, we are only accountable for our life and the decisions we make. At the end of your life, it's just you and the Lord. We can't blame our way out of our life choices. God is not going to discuss someone else's story with us. They will answer to that. In the same way, I can't talk about my mum's story. She did her best in that season against a lot of odds, she was a good mother in more ways than not. She had a lot to deal with, with no help and very little money. And although I can see our life as unfortunate, in some ways God graced it, and I would not change it now, even if I had the power to do so. It made me who I am and that is a child of the King, my redeemer.

At the end of John's gospel (John 21:15–23), Jesus gives instructions to Peter to care for and feed his sheep – the sheep are believers; to feed them, means to teach them the word and help them grow in their relationship with God. Peter asks Jesus who will betray Him. And then he asks Jesus about the destiny of John. Jesus says, *"What is that to you?"* (verse 23). He doesn't share other people's stories with others. We are to be accountable for our life and cannot blame others before God for any of it.

Another point I find amazing in this text from CS Lewis is that just like God in our lives, Aslan was always there for Shasta. He guided and saved him, then enabled him to fulfil his purpose, against the odds. Although his journey was not easy, and his life in real danger, he was in the place he needed to be to see Aslan's will fulfilled. Despite everything he went through, Aslan was there guiding and orchestrating his life to fulfil its purpose. We will probably never know how much God has guided, protected and led us along our journeys in life. He has also brought you into situations where you meet people who are to be an important part of your life. He cares so much about you and the fulfilment of your purpose. He is a good, good Father.

14

God has a plan

After the first few weeks of struggling, the first year at Bible College flew by. It was an awesome year, meeting with God, getting into His word and spending time with Phil and so many wonderful friends. I wanted to leave after Year 1 and go back to Kenilworth to start working and serving in the church. My ADHD was kicking in and I felt I had been sitting around for long enough and the youth of Kenilworth needed me there. However, Phil believed it was right to stay for a second year and I eventually, begrudgingly, heard God and realised we both needed to stay on.

In the second year of Bible College, Phil and I got engaged. Yay! I had in my head that my mum or my mum's dad, my grandad, would walk me down the aisle and give me away at the wedding. During my prayer time I felt the Lord tell me to contact Dad and ask him to give me away. I had very little contact with him during this season of my life. I didn't even know how to contact him, where he lived or anything. I'm not sure where it came from, but I was given the number of the pub he hung out in. I called, not really expecting much but he was there. The call didn't go well as he was extremely drunk and was saying repeatedly that he didn't know me. I said to God, "I have tried, and it didn't work, so there!" But much to my annoyance, I felt God ask me to do this again. The second call was just as useless. Again, I felt God ask me to do it again. The third time he wasn't so hostile. I told him about Phil, that I was getting married in the summer and God had told me to ask him if he would consider walking me down the aisle and giving me away. He said no at first as he didn't want to go in a church building, but he eventually gave in (much to my disappointment).

Our wedding day was amazing. It was God-filled and a full-on celebration. Dad walked me down the aisle and yes, he was a little drunk and was shaking more than me, but he did it. I thought very little of it at the time as I was just obeying God but it actually shifted something between us.

On the day we came home from our honeymoon I got a call from Dad. For the first time ever in my life, he had called me. He said he was proud of me and the wedding day was special. I cried. I could see the wisdom of God in telling me to ask Dad to give me away. It was to create a platform of a happy memory and to begin to repair a relationship that was, at best, in tatters and hanging by a thread. It gave us something to talk about that was positive for once. Dad asked if Phil and I would like to meet for a drink in the pub that weekend. We did and it was OK. We kind of became friends again. We met up with him occasionally (always at the pub and once at my mum's for my 21st birthday). God's tender hand was at work. He is such a good and faithful God. A year later Dad became very ill with lung and liver cancer. We all knew he would die because of the way he had treated his body for so many years. He was re-married at this point. His new wife didn't much like me or my sister and clearly had her own issues, which made things a bit awkward for us, but God was still in control.

15

Betty

In the Baptist church in the 90s there was a faithful Christian called Betty. She worked with alcoholics and had a heart to see them set free. She had met my dad when my parents were still together, and he liked her, which was unusual as she was a Christian. Probably a good ten years had passed, and we had lost touch with Betty. Then one day out of the blue, Betty heard God tell her to find Keith (my dad) and lead him in a prayer of repentance and salvation to God. She felt led by God to take a dictaphone with her, but she had no idea how to find him. She managed to get hold of my mum who managed to find his address.

Betty showed obedience to God in what He was saying to her. She drove around to my dad's house, with no warning and knocked on the door. From what I gather, my dad's new wife answered and reluctantly let her in. She went over to my dad and spoke with him. He was in a lot of pain that day, but he was sitting up on the sofa, still fully there mentally. She made a bit of small talk with Dad and had to jog his memory of how they had met on the one occasion in the past. Anyway, to get to the point, Betty led my dad in a prayer of repentance and he gave his life to Jesus. We have the heart-breaking recording on a tape cassette from Betty's dictaphone, which I still have to this day. My dad, through his tears, sincerely repents and commits himself to Jesus. He also apologises for the way he treated us, which was so freeing to hear. It's absolutely amazing. My dad hated God with a passion in the past, you could not talk about God around him as he would have fits of absolute rage and anger.

Betty

Once when I was a child, he was assaulted and nearly died. When he was recovering, he had told me that during the assault he had gone to hell. He relayed the experience that he was falling, down and down into darkness, surrounded by pure evil. He heard people groaning and saw in the darkness creepy figures and voices telling him to be quiet. Even so, despite this experience, he still did not want to surrender his life to Christ. He was so full of pride. The threat of eternity in hell and separation from God did not sway him to repentance at that point. This story proved to me he was very aware there was a God and a devil as well. He just chose to be proud and carry on living a life to please himself.

Anyway, that night through Betty's obedience to God, my childhood prayer was answered. My dad became a Christian. He gave himself to Jesus, repented and accepted Jesus as his Lord and Saviour. About 5am we had a missed call from my dad's house. On the voicemail there was nothing but the muffled sound of my dad's voice. It was about 10am on a Saturday when my mum called to tell us Dad had been taken into hospital, he seemed to have lost his memory and was now bed bound and unable to speak, due to some sort of stroke. He died not long afterwards. Whilst he was in hospital, he thought Mum was still his wife. It was really sad. I praise God that despite the past, my dad is in heaven with Jesus and one day I will see him again.

16

The children

Phil and I got married in July 2001. Despite being in the middle of summer, it absolutely lashed down with rain almost the whole day. There were even a few hailstones in the morning. However, the day was amazing, surrounded by all our family and friends in Horsham, West Sussex. We had a wonderful two-week honeymoon in the Dominican Republic, but by the end of it I was ready to get home to start building our married life and, of course, I wanted to open all our wedding presents.

We started to try for a baby in 2002 as I desperately wanted a child. However, months and years went by. Month after month became more and more devastating. The doctors help once you have been trying for a year or so. In the second year of trying, we started the awful trials of tests and examinations to work out why we were unable to conceive naturally. During this tough time, Phil and I both received visions from God about the future. We both saw a beautiful boy with blond hair and so we knew we would have children and the first would be a boy.

In 2004 we had a visiting speaker at our church called Doctor James Maloney. He was an evangelist and had a healing ministry. I don't remember the word he shared, but he invited people forward for prayer who needed healing. I went forward. He asked me what I wanted. I fell to my knees and without telling him the problem I unashamedly cried out, "I just want a baby!" He helped me to my feet and with Phil by my side we prayed, surrounded by my church family. James Maloney prophesised over me: "God is healing the scar tissue

The children

stopping you from conceiving and in the name of Jesus you will produce eggs. You will be pregnant this year."

Sometime in early June, Phil and I went to the hospital to find the outcome of our tests. We were sitting in a small side room with the doctor as she explained all the reasons I would not be able to conceive and how we would need to address the situation. It turned out I had such bad scar tissue from endometriosis that the eggs could not attach. They also discovered, through the three months of tests, my eggs were duds. There was no way in the natural realm I could possibly conceive. The only hope the doctor could offer was to keep me in hospital and pump me full of hormones to make me produce eggs and then we would be given three attempts at IVF.

They wanted to keep me in hospital for a week or two as the hormones would make me very ill. This would have meant time off work (which we could not afford) and a horrific time physically. The words the consultant said to us sounded so familiar, as we had already heard them before but in a reverse order. "God is healing scar tissue," (said the preacher) "you have such bad scar tissue the eggs can't attach" (said the doctor) and "you will produce eggs and you will conceive" (said the preacher) "We will need to keep you in hospital and put you on medication to make your body produce eggs" (said the doctor).

There was little to no hope in the natural realm, but with God all things are possible, because He isn't limited to the natural.

Little did I know that whilst we were being told we would not be able to conceive naturally, I was already pregnant. God had already put our wonderful son, Max Gabriel (meaning 'Greatest Gift of God') in my womb. The same boy we both saw in our dreams years before.

17

Miracle-working God

A week or so later, still oblivious to the fact I was pregnant, we were out shopping, looking for garden furniture for my birthday. I can remember what I was wearing, the weather and the smell of the air that day! I looked down at my tummy, and felt God say, "You are pregnant." I presumed this was not from God as I had started my period in the morning and had a tampon in and taken tablets for the pain. However, despite this I really wanted to buy a pregnancy test as I just couldn't shake the feeling that God was talking to me. I told Phil what I had heard and we agreed to get a test.

We went to Sainsbury's and bought a pregnancy test, as I had done so many times over the previous three and a half years, but this time it felt different. It wasn't just blind optimism. We came home, I did the test and praise the Almighty God, I was pregnant. It was one of the best days ever! We were so happy we just hugged and cried and laughed. I called my friend at the time who was a GP and she told me to try and distract myself and do another test in a couple of hours to make sure. We were trying to sort out the garden out at that time, so I carried on cutting back the hedge with the electric hedge trimmers. I was so distracted in my thoughts I accidentally cut through the electrical cable. There was a massive bang and it tripped the switches in the house as I nearly blew myself up! Anyway, we did another test a couple of hours later and I was definitely pregnant. This was a Saturday so I couldn't wait to get to church the next day. We announced the amazing news, and all our church family rejoiced with us.

Miracle-working God

We knew this baby was a gift from God and all would be well. There was no fear of loss, despite all the warnings the midwives gave, and even though I continued to have a little bleed every month. We just kept on thanking God for our little blond boy. The name Max means 'Greatest' and Gabriel means 'Gift of God' because he really was the most wonderful gift from God, out of possibly the hardest time in both of our lives. Nine months after his birth we conceived our precious princess, Gracie Malise. We weren't expecting this to happen so quickly but were so pleased it did. Gracie means 'Gracious' and Malise means 'Servant of Jesus'. They both live up to their names and are God-filled amazing gifts from God. Before I conceived, during the difficult years of trying, I promised God that if I was ever to have children, I would always give glory to Him for them. So, I would imagine any of you reading this who know me – whether you are a Christian or non-Christian – already know this story. I believe this is also why I conceived before the treatments could go ahead – so God can have all the credit and glory and not the medical team, although they, too, were amazing. To God be the glory forever.

Libby and Phil on their wedding day, 14 July 2001

Libby with Gracie (3 months) and Max (20 months) in October 2007

Photo credit: Libby's sister via adoption, Esther Packer

Part Three

Surfacing of addiction

"No great wisdom can be reached without sacrifice."
                    The Magician's Nephew, CS Lewis

18

Demons in the closet

As life continued and the children grew up, although they are an absolute blessing, the more 'demons in the closet of my heart' started showing their ugly faces. I had always enjoyed a drink but the older the children got, the more I drank.

I struggled when making comparisons to my life growing up. I put expectations on them that they should be as I was, in the sense of being able to do things early, like washing, cooking and cleaning. It was also difficult seeing how amazing Phil was with the children and realising I didn't have that growing up. I had fears I was like my dad, in the sense that I wanted to batter them every time they did something wrong, and so much more. At the time, I didn't fully realise what these issues were and so I was unable to deal with them rationally or even take them to God. I would just get angry, annoyed, depressed and overwhelmed. I would end up taking it out on Phil and the children without any explanation of what I was feeling. It would cause me to turn to alcohol to numb the feelings I didn't like, want, or understand.

I had help over the years from Phil, my pastor and his wife but they could only help in areas I opened up about. To everyone else, I only showed what I wanted them to see. For over a decade I used alcohol as a sedative to deal with trauma I didn't understand. The very thing I hated, alcoholics, I had now inadvertently become. I now understand that if you are an addict, it usually stems from some sort of trauma, which is why we really shouldn't judge. My attitude of hatred for addicts came from a childlike way of thinking. I thought no one was a true addict, you should just stop being selfish and stop it. It's hard with addiction and other similar entrapments as they grow subtly – a little here and a little there until you are in too deep to get out. The devil doesn't come to you in his full-on shiny red devil outfit when everything is going well. He sneaks up on you and drip feeds you lies, with temptations, until you give in.

Initially when the children were young, I struggled to be cooped up indoors all day and felt myself going insane. I had cabin fever and was desperate for Phil to get home so I could feel human again. After a while I set up my own cleaning business, which was perfect to fit in around nursery and school pick-ups. I was good at it, and with no advertising I built up a great reputation. I had been responsible for housework from a very early age, often under the overbearing expectation of my dad, so I was very good at cleaning. As I became more successful, I was given access to big, posh houses in the middle of nowhere and would spend most of my days with no contact with other people. Obviously, I would see Phil when he got home from work and I have always had people round in the evening, but I basically felt isolated and bored, and I ended up really depressed. I didn't want to kill myself, but I did want to disappear. I felt everyone would be a lot better off without me. I had hours where I lost time. I would realise I had been just staring, sitting or standing in the same spot for ages. I was close to having a serious psychological breakdown. I went to the doctor and was put on anti-depressants. These helped but I didn't want to stay on them forever, but my head felt clearer and I wasn't losing time stuck in my own head any more.

The drinking continued to creep up but it was only once the children were asleep. I was, and still am, always on the go. It's partly the ADHD but also partly my personality. Sometimes it's hard to switch off. I have an inbuilt need to work hard. My thinking is, if you want nice things, you just need to work hard to get them. Also, if you don't work, you can't eat! That is the sort of mentality I have, which mainly comes from my childhood experiences and not wanting the same for my children. I love order and control. I love having not just a clean house, garden, shed, loft and garage but immaculate ones. I'm always busy and think I'm super-woman in the amount I can achieve in a short space of time. I take on decorating and rearranging projects all the time, as I like the idea of fresh starts. I get bored way too easily. As for many of us, these are not only my gifts or superpowers, they are also my downfall. For example, if you are a good talker and communicator this is a blessing because you can create conversation in the most awkward, quiet situations but it can also be a curse and get you into trouble or annoy people. Or you might be a really laid-back person who is level headed all the time. This is a blessing as you remain calm in all circumstances and not thrown around by emotion, but again it can get you and loved ones into trouble if you sit back and do nothing or miss opportunities. You can see what I mean, I'm sure. Intelligence is great but can make you over complicate things and be over-reliant on your own thinking when God is telling you to do something out of the box. This is why we can't judge one another; we all have issues and struggles and we are all a work in process. If you think you have it all together, you could be stuck in pride.

 My point by revealing my character to you is to explain this need to have a drink. It was originally to stop me doing jobs and help me chill out. Phil would often say, "Are you going to come and sit down yet?" He would work hard all day and want to spend a bit of quality time with me but I was off doing more and more jobs to fulfil the self-imposed expectation (hard-wired from my childhood) that I needed to be busy. Once I was sitting with my wine I would finally stop.

The drinking became more dangerous in later years when I wouldn't wait until the evening to drink. I would start much earlier in the day and carry on doing jobs with wine. I called it "whistling, while I work." I remember on one evening I was home on my own when Phil was working late, so I moved my daughter's bedroom from the top floor of our three-floor house to the middle floor. In my drunken, super-woman mode I moved the wardrobe, bed, drawers and so one up and down stairs on my own, whilst consuming three bottles of wine. I was so bruised the next day, I felt I could hardly move. I was on a downward spiral, but all I could think was that I was wonder-woman.

The devil whispering subtle lies and asking questions that draw us away from God is not a new thing. Just think of Eve's well-known error in the Garden of Eden. The devil didn't parade up to her, announcing who he was and tell her to disobey God. He slithered up in the form of a snake and whispered things like, "Did God really say ...?" and, "You will not certainly die." He is crafty and comes only *"to steal and kill and destroy"* (John 10:10) in an attempt to ruin our relationship with God.

CS Lewis portrays this tactic of the enemy in his book *The Magician's Nephew* when Digory has made the mistake of listening to the witch (symbolic of the devil) and entered into a conversation with her.

"Foolish boy," said the Witch. "Why do you run from me? I mean you no harm. If you do not stop and listen to me now, you will miss some knowledge that would have made you happy all your life ...

Undone

"I know what errand you have come on," continued the Witch. "For it was I who was close beside you in the woods last night and heard all your counsels. You have plucked fruit in the garden yonder. You have it in your pocket now. And you are going to carry it back, untasted, to the Lion; for him to eat, for him to use. You simpleton! Do you know what that fruit is? I will tell you. It is the apple of youth, the apple of life. I know, for I have tasted it; and I feel already such changes in myself that I know I shall never grow old or die. Eat it, Boy, eat it; and you and I will both live for ever and be King and Queen of this whole world – or of your world, if we decide to go back there ...

"But what about this Mother of yours whom you pretend to love so? ...

"Do you not see, Fool, that one bite of that apple would heal her? You have it in your pocket. We are here by ourselves and the Lion is far away. Use your magic and go back to your own world. A minute later you can be at your Mother's bedside, giving her the fruit. Five minutes later you will see the colour coming back to her face. She will tell you the pain is gone ...

"What has the Lion ever done for you that you should be his slave? ... And what would your Mother think if she knew that you could have taken her pain away and given her back her life and saved your Father's heart from being broken, and that you wouldn't – that you'd rather run messages for a wild animal in a strange world that is no business of yours?"

The witch continues to say Aslan has made Digory heartless. She claims that when Digory made a promise to Aslan, he didn't know what he was promising, so it won't matter as no one needs to know he has broken a promise. The witch talks and talks at Digory, feeding him lie after

Demons in the closet

lie, but then says something Digory knows not to be true. This gives him the strength to realise it is very likely the witch does not know about Aslan's character and intentions at all, so he fights back.

And even in the midst of all his misery, his head suddenly cleared, and he said (in a different and much louder voice):
"Look here; where do you come into all this? Why are you so precious fond of my Mother all of a sudden? What's it got to do with you? What's your game?"

The story ends with Digory fulfilling his promise to Aslan, which in turn brings about the protection of Narnia from the witch's enchantments for hundreds of years and brings healing to Digory's mother.

The devil sneaks up on you to drip-feed you lies. He will come and feed you half-truths, or two truths and one lie to make it sound more believable. For example, "You deserve a glass of wine. You have worked hard today. No one will know." He is sneaky and deceitful. The only way to discern the truth from the lies is to spend time with God. As in Digory's situation the witch tried to make out the lion only told him not to eat the fruit to wreck his chance of fun and eternal youth. And that he was untrustworthy and he wanted it for himself. All the untruths were a direct attack on Aslan's (God's) character. The more time we spend with God, reading the Bible, in worship, in meditation, in going to church and hanging out with other believers, the more we will get to know His character and therefore recognise lies and accusation. God only has our best interests at heart.

19

ADHD

I have been aware all my life I'm not normal...! I am constantly on the go but I love it. I do things like go for a 10k run, then come home and smash out a breakfast bar, wallpaper a wall, cook a roast and have the kitchen done in time to eat dinner with the family at the table. I'm constantly on the go, cleaning, cooking, decorating, working. I struggle to relax and sit still. I'm always fiddling with something and looking for things I can improve or change.

When we go on holiday or I have a day off, I love to be doing stuff, activity after activity. It takes a lot to tire me out. A while ago, I went on holiday to Cornwall and my good friends mentioned to me in love, "I think you have ADHD." At first this surprised me and I laughed about it. But after a while I realised my friend is so similar to me in the sense that he too is always on the go – he's more extreme than me. He also has ADHD and is a high-banded mental health nurse, working with clients who have ADHD with similar attributes to me. When I came home from my trip, I mentioned this new

idea to Phil and the kids. They replied, "Well obviously, we've known that for years."

Following this, I booked a face-to-face appointment with a doctor and have started the process of being officially diagnosed. The doctor has run though a questionnaire with me and is fully confident I have ADHD. I don't feel I will ever bother with medication, I'm 43 years old and have managed until now. However, I find this initial diagnosis totally validating. When I was talking to the doctor about the questions she asked me,

ADHD

everything she said helped me make sense of so much apparently senseless stuff I did and still do. She explained to me people with ADHD struggle to naturally produce dopamine. When I drink wine, it has a dopamine effect on my brain that helps to relax and chill out. Then my body and brain like the feeling as it's something nice and different, but she warned this can cause addiction, which in my case it did. Wow! She explained more and everything she said was like a little piece of the puzzle of my life slotting into place and giving me some sort of understanding. I'm not going to find my identity in this label, but man, it does explain a lot!

20

What a plonker

For a time, life ticked on. We are never far from drama and challenging circumstances, as I'm sure you're not either. As an example, I made myself very unwell for a few days, taking myself off anti-depressants simply because I felt judged by a young Christian lad after church one day. He said something along the lines of believing Christians should not take anti-depressants because they should be reliant on God. I'm not sure what his thinking behind this was, or even if there was any thinking behind it at all. However, it was enough to make me believe he could be right. Maybe Christians shouldn't take tablets to manage depression, they should just rely on Jesus. This is NOT the case at all, it's like saying I won't take a pain killer when I have a headache. We can take a tablet, but we can always trust God as well.

Like a plonker, I just stopped taking them. I remember feeling weird, lightheaded and feeling like I'm falling a lot. After the shock of coming off them overnight rather than weaning myself off them gently under medical supervision, I seemed OK. There is nothing wrong in taking medication, depression is often caused by a chemical imbalance in the brain. By taking tablets prescribed by your doctor, it can help you deal with the whole chemical imbalance, which then makes addressing other things a lot easier. You can then feel stronger to make other necessary changes to your lifestyle to have a healthier, more fulfilled life. You don't have to take them for life, just for a while, to help get 'normal' life back on track.

What a plonker

However, I'm not a doctor and neither was the Christian lad, so make sure you ask your doctor and listen to the advice. We also need to be careful what we say to people who are struggling with physical or mental issues as we can unintentionally put unnecessary pressure on people and give advice that can be harmful.

21

Alcohol addiction grows

When the children started at secondary school, my drinking got even worse. My Auntie died and she had also been an alcoholic. She had functioned for many years, like me, until she couldn't anymore, and it consumed her. I think, however, she was getting better and getting help when she died, in her sleep due to a bleed on the brain. It was a bit of a wake-up call to say the least. It's a common theme from that side of the family. It's just seen as the norm to drink a large amount of alcohol every day. It is respected amongst them and people who don't drink are seen as the strange ones. To be fair, it hasn't done some members of the family any harm to look at them. Both my Aunties were (and the last remaining one still is) beautiful and lovely people. However, my poor Nanny lost two of her children to alcohol-related issues before she died.

Like most functioning alcoholics, although I knew it wasn't normal to drink as much as I did, and despite the fact my dad and Auntie died way too young, I felt I was immune to this happening to me. We alcoholics think we are invincible. I wasn't overweight, I ate and exercised well, held down a full-time job as well as cleaning the church, all while I was grafting and growing a beauty business. I had a husband, two children, and a dog to walk as well as an immaculate house to run. In my pride and sin, I thought the good outweighed the bad and I was OK. I believed I needed to drink to function and to sleep and I justified it by saying, "We all have our faults." I also thought I wasn't harming anyone, including myself. This of course was another lie and another bar on my prison doors.

Alcohol addiction grows

My drinking got worse and worse. I hid the evidence everywhere – in the airing cupboard, wardrobe, under the sink, in my underwear drawer, in my handbag. I had some at the salon for when I worked late as I found I would get the shakes really badly after 4pm if I didn't drink. Over the weekends, holidays and days off I would have to mix wine with my orange juice to help with my withdrawals in the mornings. I would even drink before going for a run with my sister. She and Phil were the only ones who called me out on it. My sister could smell it on me despite my best attempts at brushing my teeth and using mouth wash. I would always lie because I didn't want to stop and I didn't want to talk about it. I was getting so good at lying and being deceitful.

A large part of the problem with my alcohol addiction, which I called my 'superpower' (but was more like an evil power or curse), is that I have never had a hangover. I could drink three bottles of wine and on some occasions more, get up early the next day go for a run, walk the dog, do a day's work and have no symptoms whatsoever. It sounds great, but it just plastered over the real problem and helped me hide it even more. The only effects I had were being thirsty and having shaky hands. I still have shaky hands, it's just not as bad. People would say to me, "Once you are in your 20s you will have a hangover", "Once you are in your 30s you will have a hangover", "Once you are in your 40s you will have a hangover", but it never happened. So, the only thing physically stopping me was willpower. This obviously made stopping even harder.

22

Sin or addiction – are they the same?

If you are reading this book and you are not a Christian (don't belong to Jesus) then you may not like me calling addiction a sin. And for the unbeliever it often doesn't feel like it. However, the fact of the matter is the Bible says, *"For everyone has sinned; we all fall short of God's glorious standard."* Romans 3:23. Sin is anything that does not glorify God; anything that stands in the way of God's relationship with us; anything we think, say or do that goes against what God wants. Something that has no eternal benefit, or just satisfies our flesh (our human nature or soul life) – in thought, word or deed.

Think about the law of gravity. If you drop something it falls down to the ground. This is the law of gravity. It keeps us safe and stops us floating off into space, but also means what goes up must come down. This is like Biblical law or God's law. It's something that just is what it is. I can't turn gravity off because I don't agree with it and neither does God's law become nothing just because I want to break it and do my own thing. The Bible says *"all sin is contrary to the law of God"* 1 John 3:4.

The Bible says we are all sinners, therefore Jesus says we should not judge or condemn others, *"but let the one who has never sinned throw the first stone!"* John 8:7. Jesus totally roasted the crowd with this statement. The people were all ready to stone an adulteress to death for breaking the law, but Jesus reminded them we have all sinned.

The Bible clearly says, *"Don't be drunk with wine"* Eph 5:18 and Proverbs 20:1 says, *"Those led astray by drink cannot be wise."*

Sin or addiction – are they the same?

However, Jesus was also no party pooper. He loved a celebration and his first recorded miracle was turning water into wine. Of course, it was Jesus and the Father who created grapes in the first place.

Galatians 5:19-23 in The Passion Translation of the Bible states:

"The behaviour of the self-life is obvious: sexual immorality, lustful thoughts, pornography, chasing after things instead of God, manipulating others, hatred of those who get in your way, senseless arguments, resentment when others are favoured, temper tantrums, angry quarrels, only thinking of yourself, being in love with your own opinions, being envious of the blessings of others, murder, uncontrolled addictions, wild parties, and all other similar behaviour.

Haven't I already warned you that those who use their 'freedom' for these things will not inherit the kingdom realm of God! But the fruit produced by the Holy Spirit within you is divine love in all its varied expressions: joy that overflows, peace that subdues, patience that endures, kindness in action, a life full of virtue, faith that prevails, gentleness of heart, and strength of spirit. Never set the law above these qualities, for they are meant to be limitless."

The Bible clearly shows that any uncontrolled addictions, including alcohol, are sin and this is God's law. Like gravity it will have consequences; we can't change the law to suit us. The law is what it is. What goes up, must come down!

23

The wine witch

Every day in the afternoon/evening what I now call 'the wine witch' would whisper in my ear things like:

"Go on you deserve a drink, you have worked so hard today."

"Everyone does it, a glass of wine will de-stress you."

"You don't like puddings so this is your treat."

"If it wasn't for the wine, you'd be boring."

"You are more fun when you drink."

"You can't have people round and not drink, that's just weird."

The list went on and on. I believed the lies. Wine o'clock got earlier and earlier. Before I knew it, I would be hiding wine all over the place, at work, behind shower curtains, toilets, sinks, in cupboards or in the airing cupboard. Before Phil got home from work, I would have usually have finished a bottle already. Preparing food, making sandwiches, cleaning, walking the dog and taking kids out, already on the wine. I knew it was bad at this stage as I was lying and spending money we didn't have. The corner shop man knew the wine I drank and would have it ready for me. I was a terrible witness for Jesus. I was still full-on sharing my childhood testimony or the miracle of the children with almost everyone I met. I was leading people to Christ and praying pretty much daily with work colleagues and clients. I was truly living a double standard life.

My pastor would encourage me to fast from wine (give it up for a time) to break the habit. I would do it and hate it, and because I would do it, I would say, "See I'm not an alcoholic, because I can stop." The most googled

The wine witch

question on my phone was "Am I an alcoholic?" because I was constantly trying to justify to myself I didn't have a problem and was fully in control. During the times of fasting, I was counting down the days to when I could have my wine back again. My wine was my friend and I missed her. Phil and my pastor would buddy up with me and also stop drinking with me. They sacrificed a lot to see me free, but it never worked as I had no intention of ever fully stopping. It was so weird – when I stopped God sent me people in the exact same position and, in one case, way worse. I was helping them, encouraging and praying with them to come off the alcohol, but the whole time being desperate to get back on it myself. My will power and competitive side always came out and I liked to pretend to people – and even myself – I wasn't an alcoholic as I could stop if I wanted to.

As the years went on, the fasting made me ill. For the first three days the shakes, feelings of falling, the thirst for wine and the inability to sleep was awful. I kept this as much to myself as I could, apart from the inability to sleep, and I wanted to back my case for the need of wine. During 2018, I started to have another mental breakdown. I have no idea what caused it; just life and carrying pain from childhood stuff I never let come to the surface as I drank the feelings and emotions down.

I went to the doctor and was advised to go for counselling and was put on antidepressants again, this time with a sedative effect to help me sleep. I found I was able to sleep some nights without wine if I tried. I always under played my alcohol addiction to the doctor. I didn't go for counselling until 2021, by which time I had weened myself off the anti-depressants and wine again during another fast. My sleep was bad and I had a lot of back aches, so the doctor gave me diazepam, which I loved. I still do if I'm honest. The diazepam helped me sleep. I went to three counselling sessions and felt it really wasn't for me. I don't mind telling people my story but because of my addiction, unknown to me at the time, I was unable heal.

I became an amazing liar. By this stage the kids knew about my addiction. Phil had protected them as best as he could from what I was doing, but they could see my behaviour changing and could see the toll it was taking on Phil, and also our marriage to a certain extent. Phil and I would argue a lot because of my inability to rationalise and stay clam when drunk, which was most of the time. I don't remember what I was like, but it must have been a nightmare for Phil as he was dealing with an irrational person whose thoughts and emotions were clouded by alcohol. I did some shocking things and the kids would record me on their phones so they could show me once I had sobered up. They thought it was funny but I could be really nasty to Phil and my speech was so slurred. I started to hate myself for it, but I still continued to drink. Then I would try and fast for a while again, but I would keep ending up back in my old ways before long. For three years running, my new year's resolution was to cut back on the alcohol, but never give it up. The drinking became worse over lock down. During this time, I gained 3 stone and my mental health became way worse. Poor Phil was stuck in the house with me.

There is a passage in Romans 7:15-25 where Paul is talking about times in his life, even as a Christian, when he knows the right thing to do but for some reason he ends up doing the opposite, and doesn't know why. He finally realises it is only Jesus who holds the power to break through and help him do the right thing. Once he turned to Christ and gave his problems to Him, he wrote the words in Romans 8:1 *"So now the case is closed. There remains no accusing voice of condemnation against those who are joined in life-union with Jesus, the Anointed One."* (The Passion Translation) How anyone can say the Bible is not relevant, I don't know!

The years of addiction and the timeline are a bit of a blur. To most people reading this book who knew me during this time, they knew I had a problem with alcohol. To most, they thought nothing of it; to some, they would have judged; to some they wanted to help and to others they would have never known it to be that big a deal. But to Phil, Max and Gracie it became a bigger and bigger issue. I would bang on about the past as if the world owed me an apology. I would do my sister's head in, sharing my childhood story with her and her friends; a story she has very little record of, because her childhood in her mind was mostly fine ... ish.

I would want to forgive Mum, but would hurt her feelings constantly by bringing the past to the surface. I was stuck and my alcohol addiction had got me there. I had no idea how or why I was so stuck. Stuck, became my life, my norm. This made me so angry. Only recently Phil said to me I was unbearable to live with during this period. I was always angry, unreasonable and irrational. I remember wanting to run away so much, as long as I could still have full access to wine. I would not have cared who I left behind. Although I loved Phil, the kids, my sister, my friends, my church and job, I was so addicted that everything else became secondary to my love for wine. I would never have recognised it back then but I loved wine more than anything else in the world. More than Phil, the kids, my job, more than God and more than myself. It's a disgusting, shameful, sad and desolate place to be.

Undone

We talked about sending me to rehab in 2018. Pastor Dave investigated Christian rehab centres, but I didn't want to go as I didn't want my boss to know or Phil's mum and dad to know. I had spent so long as a functioning alcoholic I didn't want to have to face up to it all. I also felt I was letting God down by openly admitting to people I had an addiction. And even worse, a Christian with an addition. I was supposed to be a holy, new creation, not an addict. I came to believe I just needed to overcome it myself. To discipline myself. Never did I think or consider I should stop and be a teetotaller for the rest of my life. Phil had often said to me that giving up completely was the only way to move forwards but I didn't hear it because I didn't want to.

Part Four

Restoration

"If I find in myself a desire which no experience in this world can satisfy, the most probable explanation is that I was made for another world"

Mere Christianity, CS Lewis

24

Set free

On the 25th April 2022, we went round to our good friend's house to celebrate his birthday. Over the course of the evening, I drank loads. I had already been drinking before I left as well. When we got home, I was hammered but walked into the house saying, "I know I shouldn't drink anymore but I'm going to," so I probably drank another bottle. I was very drunk and I fell asleep soon after.

The next day was Sunday and time for church. I got up and said sorry to God, Phil and the kids and went to church. During the prayer meeting I became completely overwhelmed by the love of God towards me. I find it hard to put into words. For the first time I felt truly repentant, I really felt like I was at rock bottom and had totally let God, my family and myself down, but instead of condemnation for my drunken behaviour, I felt this overwhelming sense that God had totally UNDONE me with his love.

I hadn't been asking for anything in particular, but He had unravelled me in forgiveness and grace. His intensity burned deep. It was only minutes, but this amazing and tangible presence, intensity and all-consuming love were running all over me. In that moment nothing else mattered, all I wanted to do was be still and stay in the moment, just me and God – safe, and totally loved.

God had asked me time and time again, "Do you love Me more than wine?" I would always answer, "Yes, of course." But God knew my heart, even better than I did. I loved wine more than Him, but couldn't admit it to myself or Him. In this moment at church His question came to me again and I finally answered truthfully. I

Set free

realised the only way I would be able to truly prove my love for God and be able to love Him more than wine, would be to promise to never drink alcohol again. I realised I was like all the people in the Old Testament, repeatedly stuck in an eternal circle of sin. Repenting and sinning, repenting and sinning, again and again, over and over. I was wasting my life on a merry-go-round of sin, living a life in between worlds, sitting on the fence of life. It was getting harder to balance and more and more uncomfortable. I became aware the addiction was killing me and destroying everything and everyone I loved.

In that moment, clarity and clear thinking descended on me like a gentle all-consuming, loving dove. It's so hard to explain and to give justice to. I basically encountered God Almighty in His love and mercy. He led me in true repentance and set me free.

25

True repentance

True repentance can only come by the grace of God. In ourselves we can have the best intentions to do better and try harder but when God is on it, He gives us the ability to succeed and live a righteous life – to continuously walk with the Lord. So often in life, there's not a 'magic wand' moment, we must walk through some tough stuff, allowing God to sanctify us in the process. To repent means to turn away. Eerdmans Bible dictionary includes this definition of repentance, "In its fullest sense it is a term for complete change of orientation involving a judgment upon the past and a deliberate redirection for the future."

Throughout the Old Testament we see God and the Old Testament prophets calling individuals or Israel to repent, turn from their sin and walk a life in obedience to God's holy commandments. People would be made aware of their sinfulness, and do rituals. They would wear sackcloth and ashes or tear their clothes. This showed they were sorry. Then they would sacrifice an animal, because the consequence of sin is death and can only be made right by the shedding of blood. Finally, they would set their minds and hearts to obey the Lord's commands. They would usually do something radical to demonstrate they were serious about their repentance, like destroying idols and tearing down any pagan altars. They would then cut themselves off from anything that was birthed from idol worship (false god stuff). Most of the time the Old Testament people would do this because they recognised and saw physically that people who obeyed and followed the ways of the Hebrew God, the only living and real God, actually had successful lives, they were wise, protected and multiplied in number and crops. The physical out working of pagan worship, and not obeying God and living a life seeking after wealth, lust, greed and self-indulgence only led to them seeing the back of God. This meant they were no longer under his wing of protection and therefore brought calamity and destruction upon themselves. In Joel 2:12 the Lord says,

That is why the Lord says,
  "Turn to me now, while there is time.
Give me your hearts.
  Come with fasting, weeping, and mourning.
Don't tear your clothing in your grief,
  but tear your hearts instead."
Return to the Lord your God,
  for he is merciful and compassionate,
slow to get angry and filled with unfailing love.
  He is eager to relent and not punish.

The theme of repentance continues all the way though the New Testament as well. Repentance is not an out-of-date subject or just something you had to do under the old ways. It's needed for us to keep growing in our ongoing salvation. Jesus Himself says we must turn from our sin, for the kingdom of Heaven is near. Matthew 4:17 and Matthew 3:8 tell us to prove by the way we live that we have really turned from our sins and to God. As Christians, we are called to live differently and to prove it in how we live our lives.

To repent of your sin, to ask for and receive forgiveness is totally amazing. We are so privileged to have access to righteousness in Christ. To be made holy and pure, to be given a clean slate and a fresh start. Yes, sin often has consequences that need putting right or working through, but you can start by saying sorry to God and believing He has forgiven you and done a nice deep clean inside you. It's amazing the freedom we are given and the grace to move and grow in Him. It is also amazing to know every day can be a fresh start for us as believers. All we need to do is say sorry and try afresh to walk in alignment with God and His word. If you ask, I know He will do this for you. He is a faithful, awesome God. He cannot lie. It says in His word, *"Come close to God, and God will come close to you"* James 4:8. Draw close to Jesus right now; put down the book and breathe in His presence. Ask Him to help you. And let him pour His love on you. You are so loved by Him. Receive His forgiveness. Verse 10 continues to say, *"Humble yourselves before the Lord, and he will lift you up in honour."*

26

My promise to God

In that moment at church, before the main meeting even started, I made a covenant with God. I promised I would never drink alcohol again. I immediately realised I needed to declare this out loud, so I walked over to my dear friend and said through my tears and my heartbreak, "I have promised God I will never drink again." I then said it to Phil and Gracie. Phil was so delighted. He had given up alcohol months before to try and encourage me to stop and to support me. I had to hide in the church kitchen as I was crying uncontrollably and didn't want to have to explain to anyone else in church that I'm crying as I got so drunk last night and for the last 15 years on and off I've been a functioning alcoholic. The whole church now knows, by the way.

However, I'm a bit embarrassed to say the reason I was crying was not because I was sorry, although I was. I was crying because of grief. I was grieving the loss of my friend 'wine'. This is no exaggeration; I spent the whole day crying about the fact I would never drink again. I was utterly heart broken. My relationship was such a deep-rooted part of me. It was like losing an actual person. I was upset I would never get to taste and feel the effects of alcohol again. It was the loss of a dear friend and crutch in my life, gone forever. That night, however, I slept like a baby, so deeply, which had never happened without alcohol before.

The next day was Monday, which was my day off. By the time I woke up, Phil and the kids had gone to school and work. I opened my eyes and realised I was FREE. Totally set free. I knew I would never drink again. I would never spend the whole day desperate to get home to open the wine. I would never forget special times or events due to drunkenness. I would never show myself up with drunken behaviour. I would stop failing God in this area. I could stop failing Phil and be a better wife and mother to the children. I could rebuild, restore and grow and let God heal me completely.

I had no cold-turkey symptoms. God saved me from this and I sleep well nowadays. I lost 3 stone – yes 3 stone – in weight. The same amount I put on during lockdown, even though I discovered a love for puddings which I never had before. My fingernails, skin, eye lashes and hair became healthier than ever. The whites in my eyes became whiter; I didn't have the jowly, puffy look to my face. I felt fitter, stronger and had more energy than ever.

27

Piff, paff, puff

I can honestly say I longed for wine every day for the first few months. It has got easier day by day, but I still want it even now. God has not magicked the desire away, even though I wish He would. There is a story in 2 Kings 5 that talks about a mighty warrior called Naaman. He was the king's commander of the army and had leprosy. Naaman heard via his servant there was a prophet in the country called Elisha, who could heal people. Naaman went to the prophet, with the king's blessing, and took many amazing gifts with him, so he could buy his healing from the man of God. When Elisha saw him coming, Elisha sent a messenger out to meet him with the instruction to go and dip himself in the river Jordan seven times. This would then result in his skin being restored and he would be healed. Naaman became very angry and in my opinion, rightly so. He had travelled for nearly 200 days to get to this destination, as the journey was around 1,600km.

I can understand why it caused offence that Elisha didn't bother to go out and greet Naaman, showing gratitude for all the gifts. Instead, he sent his servant out to meet him! However, for Naaman to receive his healing, he had to humble himself and do something he did not understand. He, like me, wanted God to come before him with a magic wand and go "piff, paff, puff" and his skin be healed from the disease immediately. I wanted – and still want – God to magic away this desperate thirst for wine, but it hasn't happened. What the prophet asked of Naaman was not hard or even a big deal, but it was outside his idea of how healing should be done. Instead of being angry and offended by Elisha, he should have immediately followed his instructions and dipped seven times in the river. Naaman nearly walked away, went home ill and probably been exiled from his home and forced to live with other lepers – because of anger, offence and pride. Fortunately, he didn't. He was encouraged by his friend to do as the prophet had said, dip in the water seven times and he was healed.

There are so many lessons to be learned from this story, but the one I want to draw on is that God is a Sovereign, Almighty God whose thoughts are beyond our thoughts and His ways are far higher than our ways. He doesn't just magic temptations, sickness and pain away all the time. Sometimes there are some instructions we need to follow, some disciplines we need to practise, and some worldly or fleshy desires we need to lay down at Jesus's feet. Some of the time we won't like them, but we need to understand God puts in place rules, commandments, principles and instructions. Not to restrict us or be a party pooper, but ultimately to bless us, free us and make our lives better, so we can have a closer relationship with Him as unhindered by sin as we can. We are all a work in progress.

I and my family love to watch *Married at First Sight* on TV and quite often we see couples who are falling in love who then go and blow it because of pride and selfish ambition. It's easy to see when you are watching. You find yourself screaming at the TV screen, "It's not worth it! Say you're sorry!" This is probably what the Holy Spirit is saying to us when we are messing up, "It's not worth it, your eternity depends on this, your quality of your short life here on earth depends on this! Just say you're sorry and humble yourself before God, be forgiven and restored."

Piff, paff, puff

We will always have something we are working on in our character, in relationships, in needs and wants because we are a work in progress. God is transforming us from one degree of glory to another (2 Corinthians 3:18). God is a sovereign and fair God but I think we need to look to Him in relationship and adoration more than for what he can do for or give to us. This extract from *The Magician's Nephew*, is a great creative example of how we should come to God on His terms and not ours:

"Son of Adam," said Aslan. "Are you ready to undo the wrong that you have done to my sweet country of Narnia on the very day of its birth? . . .

"Yes," said Digory . . .

"But please, please – won't you – can't you give me something that will cure Mother?" Up till then he had been looking at the Lion's great feet and the huge claws on them; now, in his despair, he looked up at its face. What he saw surprised him as much as anything in his whole life. For the tawny face was bent down near his own and (wonder of wonders) great shining tears stood in the Lion's eyes. They were such big, bright tears compared with Digory's own that for a moment he felt as if the Lion must really be sorrier about his Mother than he was himself.

Digory had brought the witch into the newly-created land of Narnia. He chose to strike a bell, which he felt was wrong but did it anyway. In doing this he awakens the witch, who then entered our world causing chaos. Digory's mother is dying back in our world and of course he is desperate to see an end to her suffering and knows Aslan has the power to heal her – or send him home with something that will heal her.

Digory had been looking to the hand of God; what God can do for him. He was hoping Aslan would piff, paff, puff, with his magic wand to heal and restore his mother. Back in our world, we know this is what God could do, but as in so many cases, this would only meet the immediate need. As time goes on would you remember this to be the hand of God providing for you? Would you give credit to Him? Would you acknowledge it was God? Or would you give credit to medicine, doctors, friends, family, money, good luck, a higher energy, power, mother nature or your own goodness?

I wanted God to piff, paff, puff, my alcohol addiction away. I even wanted Him to make me have a hangover – giving me something that would make stopping drinking easy. Make me hate the taste of wine, please. He could have easily done this, but I would have definitely have given credit to myself and my will power. That would have discredited it being a miraculous healing from God. I would never have gone on a healing journey with Him.

By God not always simply providing what we think we need straight away, we go on a journey of learning instead. As Digory investigated Aslan's face (the face of God) he realises Aslan is sympathetic to his longing for his mother's health to be restored and her life to be spared. When he looks into his face, he learns Aslan's character in that moment, and his ability to understand human emotion and weakness. Digory realises there is something more about this lion than what he can do for him. When we look to the face of God, we look to His character, His personality and His Godliness, but also His ability to identify with our humanity. He knows this life is hard and painful sometimes and when we look into His face, we are looking for relationship. When we look into His face, we are asking to know Him and not simply asking what

Piff, paff, puff

He can do for us. The hand is what provides, but the face is relationship.

As it turns out, Digory gets his provision, and his mum is healed. However, Digory also grows in his understanding of Aslan's character, will and purpose for his life. He grows in his relationship with Aslan. As we look into the face of God rather than just at His hands, we are asking to go in relationship with Him, which is a journey with God.

28

Life is never easy
(but God will help you make
the right choices)

In the months after I gave up alcohol, we had a lot to deal with. We had a dodgy builder who ran off without completing the job and took our money, which was a gift from my in-laws in the first place. It was a horrid season. We also had extended challenging family situations, and just life in general to fight through, without wine.

I had to learn to enjoy family life without wine, all over again. Even things like time in front of the TV without wine took getting used to. I had to discipline myself to read books before bed to slow my mind down after a crazy day of work. I had to socialise, go on holiday, go to weddings and parties without wine. Every normal everyday thing became a learning curve. The biggest one was learning to deal with emotions again; letting the feelings bubble up to the surface without drowning them out with wine. Not just bad or negative emotions, but the good ones as well.

It sounds crazy, but I want to be as honest as I can. If you are on a similar journey, thinking about starting a healing journey from addiction or if you want to relate to others and help them on a similar journey, then this is for you. Even things like love, having fun and intimacy with your partner! When you are no longer under the influence of alcohol, it all becomes very new, hard and raw. Especially after 15 years of dependency.

Life is never easy

"You met the Witch?" said Aslan in a low voice which had the threat of a growl in it.

"She woke up," said Digory wretchedly. And then, turning very white, "I mean, I woke her. Because I wanted to know what would happen if I struck a bell. Polly didn't want to. It wasn't her fault. I – I fought her. I know I shouldn't have. I think I was a bit enchanted by the writing under the bell.

"Do you?" asked Aslan; still speaking very low and deep.

"No," said Digory. "I see now I wasn't. I was only pretending." There was a long pause. And Digory was thinking all the time, "I've spoiled everything. There's no chance of getting anything for Mother now."

The Magician's Nephew, CS Lewis

In life, God gives us choices. Sometimes we make the right choice and, in some situations, we make the wrong one. As we grow, we need to mature and learn not to blame others or make excuses for the times we make the wrong choice. In the above text, Digory starts to make excuses for why the witch was awoken. However, when faced with the all-knowing Aslan he realises he needs to give up and be honest with himself and Aslan (God). God is a redeemer and although we frequently mess up, all that is required of us is an honest conversation with Him and a soft and repentant heart. Sometimes we will have to make the effort and put in the required work to mend the situation, which is similar to Digory. He gets sent on a quest to redeem the mess he previously made. However, in the meantime Digory hasn't spoiled anything. In the story, Aslan not only enables Digory to fulfil his quest by giving him all he needs to do it, but Digory also receives the desire of his heart, the healing of his mother. I love the way CS Lewis portrays God though Aslan. To me, as I develop in my relationship with God, I recognise more and more how similar God is to Aslan. I have written about when God asked me if I loved wine more than Him. I would always answer with, "Of course not, Lord!" which I had pretty much convinced myself to be the truth. So, although I was clearly lying to God with my answer, I was also lying to myself. I have come to learn God, like Aslan, is in the above quote. He asks questions He already knows the answer to so we will realise and acknowledge our need for Him. When we do this, He can then restore and put it right. He asked me a question recently when I was reading a Psalm, seemingly from nowhere. Psalm 99:4 says, *"Mighty King, lover of justice, you have established fairness."* I heard the Holy Spirit almost whisper to me, "Libby do you believe I am a lover of justice?" I went to say, "Of course God," but then I checked myself and realised I didn't always truly believe that and I knew in an instant what God was getting at deep in my heart. So, I said sorry and asked God to give me a heart that believes He is just.

When our dodgy builder ran off, leaving us with an unfinished job we had paid for, we ended up taking him to Court and winning. However, I feel we never received true justice because he didn't pay back. He probably never will pay us what the Court has asked of him. In a sense we have had half of the justice given to us. I know this sort of thing goes on all the time. I am coming to terms with the fact that God is just, and although I haven't seen the fulfilment of a horrible situation turning out as I wanted it to, I believe God is a God of justice.

Jesus asked similar questions to His followers throughout the New Testament, like to Simon Peter, *"Who do you say I am?"* Matthew 16:15.

Life is never easy

God calls out to Adam and Eve in the Garden of Eden, *"Where are you?"* (Genesis 3:9). God knows the answers to His questions but likes us to realise and learn something from them. It is all about establishing a relationship.

Digory learns more about Aslan's character from his encounters with him. As we develop more of a relationship with God and spend time with Him, we learn more about His character. When we learn about the character of God, we become better people because we become more Christ-like. We become like the people we choose to hang out with – the more we hang out with the Lord, the better and more Christ-like we will become.

29

Phil's story

My story with Libby starts in 1999 after I finished university and felt God calling me to Bible College. As a teenager there were three things I told God I never wanted to do: be a missionary, be a teacher and go to Bible College. It's funny how God works in our lives as He prepares us and leads us into His plans and purposes, even when they are in stark contrast to our own plans. Hence, I spent five weeks in Medellín, Colombia sharing God and coaching football to street children as well as teaching English to children and adults in the local church and preaching at the Bella Vista prison, which was an experience I will never forget. Also, at the time of writing I have been a PE Teacher in Coventry for 20 years. There's a lesson in there somewhere about not writing anything off when God is in control of our plans.

So that brings me to the final thing I never wanted to do, which was go to Bible College. One day I had a migraine after getting elbowed in the head during a football match. I slept all day until about 10pm when I got up to watch *Match of the Day*, but then couldn't get back to sleep. For some reason I started reading a Christian magazine my parents had in the lounge. I found an advert for Kingdom Faith Bible College and felt God was telling me I needed to go there. So, I applied and got accepted for an autumn start later that year. It was on the first day I was told by someone working in the college they had never advertised in that particular magazine. God really does work in mysterious ways.

October came and I started at the college, not knowing anyone or even anything about Kingdom Faith

Phil's story

Church. I was 21, fresh out of uni and didn't have a clue what to do with my life. I made a commitment to God to give Him this year of my life wholeheartedly, to do whatever He wanted and I would not even consider looking for a girlfriend or pursuing any romantic relationships. Again, it's funny how God's plans are not our plans, although I'm sure He appreciated my sincerity and desire to meet with Him.

College started with a meet-and-greet session with all the other new students as well as the 2nd-year students and staff. I remember seeing Libby (or Diane as she was known back then) from behind and noticed how bouncy she was and then she turned round to reveal her bright smiley face. I didn't speak to her as I am quite a shy person and the whole situation of the session was already hard work, let alone trying to make small talk with individuals.

However, God had his hand upon us and brought us together at the back of a few meetings. We were both struggling to keep up with the intensity of the worship and prayer, especially when everyone else seemed perfectly at ease with it all. With some intervention from the college pastor (some of which will never be found in any 'How To' manuals) we both had a breakthrough moment and started really moving on with God and enjoying college life. Significantly, God had used this time to bring us closer together and we started to build a really strong friendship that would ultimately become a strong marriage, built on the foundations God had laid in those early days and weeks together.

On the Friday of the first week, we and several other students walked up the road to the local pub (yes, a pub during Bible College) to take a breather from the pressure cooker life at college. It was here Libby and I first spoke about our upbringings. When I say we spoke, what I actually mean is Libby spoke for about an hour and a half while I listened and asked the occasional question to show I was interested – which I really was, by the way. She spoke of her ordeals as a child in an abusive household, not just from physical abuse but also neglect and emotional abuse, which often go unnoticed. I was astounded by her story and also how normal she seemed, despite everything she had endured in her short life. It certainly made my upbringing seem quite boring, although I am very grateful to my parents for bringing me up in a loving, God-filled environment and always supporting me. Libby's story seemed like something out of a book (ironically), but I was also intrigued by her perspective on a lot of the issues she had faced. She only held resentment towards her dad, despite being left in that abusive household for years until she had to find a way to break the cycle of abuse.

Libby and I spent more and more time together and it was clear God was doing something special between us. We grew closer in friendship and submitted our relationship to a wonderful college pastor called Frank Hottenbacher. He met regularly with us and encouraged us to keep fixing our eyes on God and trusting Him with our lives and future together. This was so important to us, especially in the intense atmosphere of Bible College, which was an equally amazing and tough two years. Then on 14th July 2001 Libby and I got married in Horsham and had our reception at the Bible College. It was so special for us with our families and friends, new and old. We felt called by God to move to Kenilworth where Libby lived previously, to be part of her church and get involved with leading the youth work. This all happened fairly quickly, and we enjoyed becoming part of the church as a newly

Phil's story

married couple. We then entered into the period of heartache and then miracle of waiting for and having our two wonderful children, who are such a blessing from God. During those early years of marriage, it was hard going as we both wanted children very much and each month, we were faced with the disappointment of not being pregnant. However, looking back, I can see how God had his hand upon us and we really relied on Him, as it says in the Bible, *"a triple-braided cord is not easily broken"* Ecclesiastes 4:12. God, Libby and I were an unbreakable team when we kept our eyes on Him.

As the children started to grow, so did Libby's interest in alcohol. This was never the start of the problem; it was how she often dealt with the underlying problems buried from her childhood abuse. As we were growing as a family and going through the tough times most parents face with young children, it put us under strain. This was magnified by the fact that the only family we had within a hundred miles was Libby's younger sister, who was in her early 20s and training to be a nurse. She was able to babysit every now and again and was really helpful when our second child was born as she looked after Max while we were at the hospital with Gracie. However, apart from Anita, we had no local family. I had moved away from my parents in Essex and Libby's mum moved to Africa weeks after Max was born. These were tough times and understandably put a strain on our relationship, but we kept looking to God and He kept bringing us through.

Libby was a stay-at-home mum until Gracie started school, but great as this was for the children to have her around so much, it took a toll on Libby as she suffered from cabin-fever. So, she got an evening job to help with the finances, but also to get her out of the house and talking to people over the age of 3. She started drinking more and more, though, to help her cope with the emotional rollercoaster of young children mixed in with ever-increasing comparisons with our family and the one she was brought up in.

At the time, I didn't fully understand what was happening inside her head. Quite often I just saw the results of it, without being able to see where the behaviour was coming from. She was very irritable, angry, seemingly dissatisfied and basically depressed. Anyone who knows the two of us will know we have completely different personalities, which is something a lot of couples experience, but I see God's wisdom almost every day with this. I am very laid back, patient and mostly easy-going, whereas Libby is very busy, active and doesn't stop moving. Sometimes we clash as a result, but actually we complement each other perfectly. If we were both like me then nothing would get done, but if we were both like Libby, we would probably have killed each other years ago.

So, during this time of personal struggle for Libby I tried to be supportive and patient with her, but I soon realised that me being me was never going to be enough. I praise God that He was with me and the kids every step of the way, because sometimes Libby's behaviour was very erratic and hostile, especially when she added alcohol into the mix. It is very difficult to reason with someone in this situation, especially when they actually have no intention or desire to give up the alcohol – as Libby didn't. At times she even seemed to want alcohol more than she wanted us. This was extremely difficult to take and many times I would pour out my heart to God, wanting to take the kids and walk away from Libby in search of an easier life, but He would always lead me to repent of any bad attitudes I had towards Libby and forgive her.

Phil's story

In my life I have frequently felt I am constantly in the background and quite like it that way. I hate parties and awkward social situations. Despite leading the church youth work for years and more recently being an elder, something has niggled away at me. I have felt my ministry is not enough for God and I don't do enough for Him. However, God spoke to me clearly during the time of Libby's struggles with alcohol. He showed me she was actually a huge part of His calling on my life – she was my ministry field. At our church, we believe all of us minister first and foremost to God, so everything we do is for and to Him. God revealed to me that I had been put in Libby's life to help her and, of course, it is not only one way. She has supported me in many ways over the years. This revelation was huge for me as it gave me a perspective of God's hand and His plans in our marriage and also for the healing He wanted to bring to Libby.

God also showed me I needed to protect our children during this time. I, with God's help, was like a buffer between them and the attacks of the enemy through Libby. I had to to keep them from being overwhelmed by the anger and harshness that came through her. In some situations, it may be God's will and common sense to remove children from the situation as I wish someone had done for Libby when she was a child, however in our situation I was always led by God to stay and fight for our family. God moves in different ways with each person, so if you are facing something similar, ask God what He wants you to do. He may tell you to get out for a time or to stay and see it through. His word will be specific to you and will bring the healing you need.

I tried many times to tell Libby she needed to stop drinking for her benefit as well as mine and our children's, but it always seemed to fall on deaf ears. It made me feel a bit offended and insignificant, but God always gave me the reassurance I needed in prayer times, even when I wanted nothing more than to walk away from it all. It's really hard to see someone you love going through addiction – and even harder when they keep on choosing it over you – but my advice to anyone in a similar position is to take it to God. He will often surprise you by showing something in your own life He wants to deal with first and then show you what to do and say, as well as giving you everything you need to stand alongside your spouse or whoever it is.

In the end, the answer from God didn't come from my nagging to give up alcohol, but as a result of me digging in and praying for Libby for a breakthrough. I can still remember Libby's teary eyes at church when she told me God had told her to stop drinking and I knew right then that would be the end. I was so happy (in contrast to Libby) and was so grateful to God for defeating this addiction in her life. I had already given up alcohol months before because I didn't want to be responsible for putting temptation in Libby's way. I still haven't had a drink to this day and probably never will again, such is my determination to support her through this.

I know Libby has often desired to have a drink since then, but she has remained strong in the Lord and His mighty power and has been faithful to her promise to God to never drink again. I'm very proud of her and so grateful to God. It is an absolute miracle to stop such a strong addiction like this with no medical or professional help or intervention. I am also immensely grateful to God, though, for the love and support He has shown to me and the children through it all. I couldn't have continued without Him guiding my paths and I encourage anyone in a similar situation to get before God, be real with Him

Phil's story

and surrender your life to Him. In doing this He will lead and guide you into His plans and purposes, which are always incredibly better than our own.

We are now over two years, at time of writing, after Libby stopped drinking and it is awesome to see her strength in God to stay strong and close to Him. It has also brought us even closer as a family. The children are almost both adults and show no negative effects of their experiences. In fact, neither of them really likes alcohol, which is another thing I praise God for. He breaks family curses and chains of addiction. Hallelujah!

"And we know that God causes everything to work together for the good of those who love God and are called according to his purpose for them." Romans 8:28

30

Telling people

Before I stopped drinking alcohol, if I met you and you were teetotal or didn't like alcohol, I would have thought you were the most boring person the world. I would presume we had no common interests and think you were a weirdo. I used to have a hot tub, which I loved having guests round to enjoy. It was great for social events, but would usually involve alcohol. I host a lot, involving alcohol. I love to cook and have great big feasts with friends and family, which involves alcohol. I thought I would lose a few friends, now that I am the boring, teetotal, weirdo.

But most people are not like me. Most people don't even notice what someone is drinking. I will still use a wine glass, but fill it with a fizzy herbal drink or tonic water. Sometimes I will just come out and tell people I'm a recovering alcoholic. With one group of friends (who are unsaved) I decided to be open and raw with them about the whole thing, as we often meet round each other's houses to eat together. They have actually been so understanding and supportive. I did, however, make the decision to still serve alcohol for any guests who want to drink. If I know people are coming around, I will have wine in the house to serve to friends and family. The fridge usually has alcopops for my son and his mates now they're over 18. The way I see it, it's me who had/has the problem, and it's me who has blown it. Therefore, it's me who misses out, not my friends and family.

I'm an honest person who carries my heart on my sleeve and I have come to a place where I own my downfalls and faults. I don't like to be judged by others but

Telling people

if they choose to judge, I think, "Oh well, it's their problem". I'm very aware I have been a bad Christian witness for many years with alcohol, and I can only apologise for that. I understand it is annoying when you know someone has an issue, yet God is still blessing them. You may look at their life and wonder why God still blesses them. However, it is wrong to judge and we rarely know what God is doing behind closed doors. Over the years I know God has blessed me so much, he is always faithful, and I have never seen his back, even though I have been entangled in the sin of addiction. Despite all of that, I still continued to be faithful in other areas. It is just as well God doesn't just cast us aside as soon as we sin, for we have all sinned and fallen short of His glory. There would be no-one left for Him to use.

31

Let's call a spade a spade

In James 1:21-25 we read, *"So get rid of all the filth and evil in your lives, and humbly accept the word God has planted in your hearts, for it has the power to save your souls. But don't just listen to God's word. You must do what it says. Otherwise, you are only fooling yourselves. For if you listen to the word and don't obey, it is like glancing at your face in a mirror. You see yourself, walk away, and forget what you look like. But if you look carefully into the perfect law that sets you free, and if you do what it says and don't forget what you heard, then God will bless you for doing it."*

In The Passion Translation, verse 24 says, *"You perceive how God sees you in the mirror of the Word, but then you go out and forget your divine origin."*

As you have been reading my story, maybe God has been pinpointing things in your heart and life you know shouldn't be there. Food addiction, or an eating disorder, lust, alcohol or drug addiction – this could be prescription tablets as well – pornography, self-harm (emotional hatred to yourself or physical harm) or similar. You will know, you will feel it. It can be other things like gossip, lying, anger, resentment, hanging out with the wrong sort of people, being in a relationship you know is not right, etc. It may also be pride or self-importance. You think you know best (better than God) what you need and what is good for your life.

Please don't be like the man James is talking about – a person who looks in the mirror and can see there's spinach in his or her teeth and walks away and forgets about it. Don't be the person who forgets God's word over and in your life. Conviction is there to benefit you. Don't forget who God says you are in his word – your divine origin. You are a child of the Most High God. Your Dad, if you choose Him as your Lord and Saviour, is God the maker of the whole entire universe.

The first thing I recommend you to do is write it down. Call it what it is, say it out load. "I struggle with . . ., this is not right, I don't want it. Help me God. Give me an undivided, pure clean heart and life." Before I gave up alcohol, I couldn't sing a lot of the worship songs. There would be lyrics like "All I desire is you," or "I live for you alone," and "Have my life as a living sacrifice." I knew I couldn't sing these things to God as I didn't want to stop drinking. Ask God to give you the desire to stop, and to stop justifying your sin. Call it what it is – lean into God. I know He will help. *"Come close to God, and God will come close to you."* James 4:8

The second thing I recommend you do is confess it out loud to someone. It can be anyone really, but definitely someone you trust, who you can be open and honest with like your husband, wife, brother, sister, pastor or friend. Tell them. This is such a hard thing to do. It can be embarrassing and will sometimes have consequences you have to face. Especially if it influences them in some way, like an affair, lying or stealing. It could result in rejection and break down in relationships but it is important to bring out into the light that which has been hidden in the darkness. This is in order to expose it and move on from it.

32

The first cut is the deepest

When I was at Bible School, Pastor Colin Urquhart gave a brilliant example for a healing illustration that has stuck with me. He said when you are sick or injured or have something that hasn't been functioning correctly, you sometimes need to have surgery to mend it. The surgeon must first cut into the patient to gain access to the affected area and then can remove or fix whatever is wrong. Often God needs to cut into the innermost parts of our lives to gain access to the root of our problems and then He can bring the healing necessary for us to walk free with Him.

It hurts just acknowledging your wrongdoing, let alone confessing it to someone, but it brings sin out of the shadows, calling it what it is. This hurts emotionally and spiritually, but will ultimately give God, the best healing surgeon in all the world, the chance to clean the wound. He can identify the root cause, remove the problem, restore, nourish, disinfect and heal you. The first cut is the deepest, but if you let God open you up, so to speak, you are in the safest hands ever. This is all while keeping in mind the end goal of restoration and healing.

This is symbolised beautifully in Chapter Seven of *The Voyage of the Dawn Treader,* where a selfish boy called Eustace walks away from his friends in pride and independence to explore, instead of helping set up camp on a new-found island. He wanders past a dead dragon, not realising the danger he is in, and enters a cave. He finds a bracelet, which he takes and puts on his arm and continues into the cave, where he falls asleep. When he wakes, he slowly becomes aware his sins, pride and

The first cut is the deepest

selfishness, have caught up with him and he has become a dragon. Although he momentarily enjoys being able to fly and breathe fire, he soon regrets drifting so far away from the person he was supposed to be. He eventually comes before Aslan, the lion who has the power to restore him, not just to who he was before, but a redeemed and healed version of himself. However, it is a painful process and involves removing the dragon skin.

"Then the lion said – but I don't know if it spoke – you will have to let me undress you. I was afraid of his claws, I can tell you, but I was pretty nearly desperate now. So I just lay flat down on my back to let him do it.

"The very first tear he made was so deep that I thought it had gone right into my heart. And when he began pulling the skin off, it hurt worse than anything I've ever felt. The only thing that made me able to bear it was just the pleasure of feeling the stuff peel off. You know – if you've ever picked the scab of a sore place. It hurts like billy-oh but it is such fun to see it coming away."

"I know exactly what you mean," said Edmund.

"Well, he peeled the beastly stuff right off – just as I thought I'd done it myself the other three times, only they hadn't hurt – and there it was lying on the grass: only ever so much thicker, and darker, and more knobbly-looking than the others had been . . . Then he caught hold of me – I didn't like that much for I was very tender underneath now that I'd no skin on – and threw me into the water. It smarted like anything but only for a moment. After that it became perfectly delicious and as soon as I started swimming and splashing I found that all the pain had gone from my arm. And then I saw why. I'd turned into a boy again."

The Voyage of the Dawn Treader, CS Lewis

Undone

At first Eustace acknowledges his horrid scaley, hard skin. He is in pain and has a desperate desire to jump into the well. He tries to get free from his skin in his own strength and it temporarily makes him feel better, but as he approaches the pool, he realises it's no good. Eustace tries three times before Aslan says, "You will have to let me undress you". Eustace is afraid, but also desperate to be better, so he agrees to let Aslan cut into him and take off the skin.

As I'm typing this passage, I'm crying. I hope you can see and feel it the way I do. This is a visual demonstration of what God did for me and can do for you too, if you allow him. Eustace tried to be free from his dragon body by himself. Being a dragon had its benefits, but also isolated him from his friends, meant he was a bit of a freak and hurt his arm so badly where he had put the bracelet on. The dragon represents sin, and in my case, it represents addiction. Eustace was at rock bottom. He wanted to change, but didn't know how to undo the enchantment that had turned him into a monster. Do you see it? Eustace's bad attitude is what led him to the cave in the first place. He put the bracelet on his arm and dreamt of a rich and wealthy future. Little did he know he had chosen a dark path – the curse of sin. For me I was struggling with the pressures of life, so I chose to drink; I thought, like Eustace, I was justified in my pride. I also turned into the dragon. I wasn't all bad; I did some good things, although I was in constant pain. I tried to rid myself of my scales time and time again, to no accord. Eustace is afraid but also desperate to be better, so he agrees to let Aslan cut into him and take off the skin.

Aslan says, "You will have to let me undress you!" When we are in deep, our own efforts and willpower are not enough. Only God can help.

The first cut is the deepest

When he looks back on the dragon skin, Eustace realises it's a lot worse than he thought. When we are in sin, we often don't see it for its true ugly self. In fact, we glamorise and justify it. Isaiah 5:20 and 22 say, *"What sorrow for those who say that evil is good and good is evil … What sorrow for those who are heroes at drinking wine and boast about all the alcohol they can hold."* We hold ourselves in the sorrow and pain of sin, through deception and pride, but God has the power to break us free from those chains (like Eustace's bracelet) of the curse (enchantment) of sin.

Sadly, the people closest to me could see what was happening to me and would even try to tell me, but I couldn't or didn't want to see it. What I desperately needed was to come to the day when I saw myself for what I was: without God in control of my life and not being surrendered to him. This happened on that day when, in desperation, I laid myself before God and allowed Christ to cut into me. Just like Eustace, it hurt but also felt good to see the scaly, dark, ugly scabs coming away. Then I allowed God to lift my weak, frail, tender body and throw it into the pool of healing. God doesn't leave us on the operating table or wandering around with raw skin, he finishes the job and brings us to full restoration through the refreshing of His healing power.

"Come, let us return to the Lord. He has torn us to pieces; now he will heal us. He has injured us; now he will bandage our wounds." Hosea 6:1

33

Orchestrated

In February 2012, when the children were six and seven years old, we were really struggling for money. I was desperately unhappy in my cleaning job and I was drinking too much, but it wasn't too out of control yet. Wine o'clock was still after the kids went to bed.

Any way, we were struggling and living out from an overdraft, getting to its limit, so would very soon have no money until pay day. I had a rich relative who I loved, and he was always on hand to help if we needed. One day he happened to have sent us a £300 cheque in the post. I got in from the daily school run and found it on the door mat. I was so happy and relieved. I popped to my neighbour's house immediately and asked if she would have the kids for an hour so I could run straight to the bank and pay the cheque in before it shut. Phil was still at work. She agreed. I was so happy; we had been sent some much-needed money and it was nice to be child-free for an hour. I threw on my trainers, put my dog on his lead and ran to the bank.

When I got to the bank, there was a massive queue. I didn't mind waiting as I was in such a good mood. There were two cashiers working that day. I knew them both as they were the cashiers when I was a dental nurse. Then it was my job on a Friday to walk to the bank to pay in the weekly 'cash-up.' We built a rapport, so I would always have a chat when I popped in.

After a good wait I got to the front of the queue. The cashier knew I had been job hunting and had an interview a week or so before, so she asked how it went. I was very much aware of the big queue behind me and I

Orchestrated

didn't want to annoy people by talking for too long. I was also aware they were all listening. Anyway, we chatted and I explained unfortunately I didn't get the job at the medical centre, but believed God had the right job out there somewhere for me.

I paid my cheque in and ran home, still in a good mood. A little later, I got a phone call on my mobile, from my bank. I thought, "Oh no". My imagination ran wild. I thought it would be the cashier who got told off for talking to me and calling to tell me next time I pop in we couldn't talk, or something similar. I answered and she said something like this, "Hi Libby, in the queue behind you was a guy who is well known in and around Kenilworth. He is a businessman, entrepreneur and a well-respected client at our bank. He doesn't advertise for staff to work for him; instead, he looks for talent and approaches them personally. He has decided from listening to you talk in the bank that you are the person he would like to work at a museum he is about to open, called the MAD Museum in Stratford. Please call him. Write his number down and give him a call."

First of all, I was not impressed, and I must admit I thought, "Weirdo" and had no intention of calling him back. But I thanked the cashier and wrote the name and number down on the envelope my relative had sent the cheque in.

I stared at the envelope and mulled his name over. "Why does his name seem familiar? I have heard this name before!" As I carried on preparing the dinner waiting for Phil to get home, it dawned on me. This was the guy who helped enable us to get a new church building. He sold a workman's yard for us to build the church when he bought the chapel from us.

Undone

When I was 18 and about to go to Bible School, our church asked God for a better building as the chapel was damp and too small. I remember praying for this, but as I was young I had very little care about the building or understanding of the politics of the whole thing. Anyway, the name of this guy rang a bell. I remembered my pastor speaking at the old chapel and in the new building, thanking God for someone with the same name, speaking blessing and salvation over his life.

I called my pastor and told him the story. He checked the mobile number I had been given and it was the same. He encouraged me to call him back and take whatever he was offering me. My pastor assured me he was a good man and a great person to have on your side. Long story short, I called him, popped into his office and had a ten-minute chat where I pretty much told him why I could not be a reception manager to a Mechanical, Art and Design Museum. I explained I knew nothing about Automata or how to run a museum, was dyslexic and had small children to take and collect from school every day. But despite all this, he still wanted me, and really would not take no for an answer! I worked at the museum for four years, and it became a massive success. After a couple of years, once it was established and running well, I basically became a glorified receptionist and got bored.

I decided to call the dental practice and see if they would like me back, now the children were a bit older and going to childcare after and before school. They did, so I left the museum and went back into dental nursing. I loved the staff at the dental practice and my bosses were fantastic. It very much felt like one big family, but again, after a few years of working there I got bored. I'm sure you recognise a pattern in my life; I get a four-year itch. My mother-in-law jokes it's a good thing I haven't got bored with Phil (that would never happen).

I was still in touch with the MAD lot and my old boss, and his nephew were good friends to me during this season of my life, so we all stayed in touch.

One day, during my lunch hour I popped into a walk-in beauty salon to get my eyebrows done. While I was there, I thought to myself, "I would be good at this job, with my people skills and creativity." Also, it would be the sort of job where I probably wouldn't get bored as it is so varied, waxing, nails, massage, etc. It was just a thought, but I spent the rest of the afternoon daydreaming about it whilst at work. Phil and I were selling our house at the time; I thought I could use a little of the equity to cover the cost of going to night school and training to be a beauty and massage therapist. Again, to cut a massive story short, during my time dental nursing my MAD boss had set up another business in Kenilworth called Little Himalaya Salt Rooms. He has severe asthma and was travelling for salt therapy to Milton Keynes. This was taking about three hours out of his day up to three times a week. As he had seen significant improvements in his breathing, he prioritised it. However, he had lots of land in Kenilworth and the know-how, so he decided to build his own salt cave, which is now a business. When I became dissatisfied at the dental practice (again) I wanted to go back and work for my old boss, but knew if I worked for the Salt Rooms it would only be weeks before I got bored because there wouldn't be enough going on to stimulate my hyperactive brain.

I had mentioned to my boss how I wanted to give up dental nursing and work for him again. But also, I quite liked the idea of retraining as a beauty therapist and using some of the equity from the sale of the house to pay for my training. He pretty much told me off like a father scolding a child. He said, "When will you stop flitting around, getting bored and actually settle down into something?" But as he is a businessman and entrepreneur with great ideas, he clearly went away and thought about it.

He called me one day and suggested we meet at the Salt Rooms, where he had a loft room that wasn't used for anything apart from storage. He suggested paying for me to do my training and using the loft space to set up what he called my 'princess parlour,' on the condition I help run the Salt Rooms as well as building a beauty business.

I have now been working as a beauty and massage therapist for over six years and manage both the salt and beauty rooms. The two years of my training were hard as I was taking over my responsibilities in the Salt Rooms as well as working 35-hour weeks at the dental practice in addition to going to college on a Monday afternoon and having two young children, a dog, moving house and leadership responsibilities in our church. But I did it, somehow, by the grace of God and with Phil's amazing support, and it's worth it. I love my job and although it's not my personal business, I treat it and see it as if it is. I have designed the salon, my leaflets, treatments and have such great clients. My boss and his son are the most fantastic bosses. I feel so blessed to have a boss that believed in me from day one, saw potential I had no idea I had and trusts me to get my head down, work hard and make the business grow.

It's so good to look back and I thank God for His hand at work orchestrating everything. Even in the bad times, God will turn it for good for those who believe and follow him. If we hadn't been in financial need, I would never have been in such a rush to go to the bank that day at that time. I would have never met my new boss. God used him to bless me and in turn I hope I have blessed him by being a hard worker and growing two businesses for him.

If I hadn't been assaulted, I would never have gone to Bible School. If I hadn't gone to Bible School, I may never have met Phil and had our two wonderful children. God is a constant. He never sleeps and is always wanting to bless His children. It says in the Bible His thoughts towards us outnumber the grains of sand. Think about that for a minute. The God of the universe, who put the stars in the sky, who made the mountains and seas, the earth and everything in it, who made you, thinks about you constantly. He thinks about you and loves you wholeheartedly. You are His child and He will go ahead of you to prepare good things for you. All we need to do in return is follow Him.

34

Do you know God? Do you want to?

The Bible teaches us we have a Trinitarian God; the Father, the Son and the Holy Spirit. All are one, but each has different characteristics.

The Father: If you have had a bad experience of a dad, it can be hard to see God as your father, but God is the perfect Father. He loves you completely, He thinks about you all the time, He wants you to be happy and successful, He loves to spend time with you and He loves to provide, protect and guard you. God the Father created us to be His children for relationship. Just as we have children to love, He created us in love and for love.

2 Corinthians 6:16 and 18: *"I will live in them and walk among them. I will be their God, and they will be my people ... And I will be your Father, and you will be my sons and daughters, says the Lord Almighty."*

Son: The Son is Jesus. The Christian faith is the only faith that can access righteous living via faith. Other religions normally require you to perform religious duties in order to live a clean and righteous life. Perhaps you must pray a certain away, abstain from certain things, dress or wear your hair a certain way, eat or not eat certain foods, etc. But Jesus gave up His place in Heaven and came to earth as a man to break this religious way of doing things. He died on a cross at the hands of sinful men, so we can access God without performance and sacramental, superficial requirements. In John 14:6 Jesus says, *"I am the way, the truth, and the life. No one can come to the Father except through me."*

In Old Testament times, when believers sinned, they would have to sacrifice an animal as atonement for sin, as sin requires death and the shedding of blood. God is so holy that without a sacrifice to atone for our sins, we would be consumed by His holiness. This is why believers say Jesus died for us, so we don't have to. I see it visually ... the cross is like a bridge creating direct access to God the Father. Jesus paid the price for all the bad and ungodly stuff you have ever done and ever will do. He did this because He loves you so much and wants the best for you. The only way to have the best life is by knowing Him. You may have money, a great family and successful job, but we were created to have a relationship with Christ. Therefore, we are all created with a God-shaped hole in us. The only way for that to be filled is with Him.

God has put a desire for eternity in our hearts. Ecclesiastes 3:11-15 says *"Yet God has made everything beautiful for its own time. He has planted eternity in the human heart, but even so, people cannot see the whole scope of God's work from beginning to end. So I concluded there is nothing better than to be happy and enjoy ourselves as long as we can. And people should eat and drink and enjoy the fruits of their labour, for these are gifts from God. And I know that whatever God does is final. Nothing can be added to it or taken from it. God's purpose is that people should fear him. What is happening now has happened before, and what will happen in the future has happened before, because God makes the same things happen over and over again."*

This is echoed in the words of CS Lewis in *Mere Christianity:* "If I find in myself a desire which no experience in this world can satisfy, the most probable explanation is that I was made for another world."

Our life on earth is short, if there is a God, there is also a devil, if there is heaven there is also a hell, if there are angels there are also demons – pick your side.

Undone

When I was a child, I dreamed of being special, powerful, having a superpower, having a rich heritage or a relationship with a superhero. Aslan is that to me. Aslan portrays the God I know and love. The God I have always known and loved. God is real, safe, powerful, terrifying, awe-inspiring, wild, untamed, mighty, alive, adrenaline-boosting, pure and tender.

This God invites us all to come before Him with childlike, wide-eyed wonder and innocence. He wants us to experience life with Him and the adventures that come along, which will only happen if we choose Him. When we do this, we have a superhero by our side.

Wild adventures are never smooth sailing, though. There will always be villains and obstacles to face. The harder the adventure, the more we will grow and flourish in His virtues. We start to become a better person and reflect God in all we do. We must allow Him to help us and guide our paths. We should choose to keep Him at the forefront of our minds, acknowledging and recognising Him on life's journeys.

> *"Look! Look! Look!" cried Lucy.*
> *"Where? What?" asked everyone.*
> *"The Lion," said Lucy. "Aslan himself. Didn't you see?" Her face had changed completely, and her eyes shone.*
> *"Do you really mean – ?" began Peter.*
> *"Where did you think you saw him?" asked Susan.*
> *"Don't talk like a grown-up," said Lucy, stamping her foot. "I didn't think I saw him. I saw him ... and he wanted us to go up where he was – up there."*
>
> Prince Caspian, CS Lewis

Lucy sees Aslan and should have followed him on the path, but she is heavily outnumbered and outsmarted by the others on the same journey. Lucy is the youngest of

Do you know God? Do you want to?

the children and sees Aslan the most throughout the *Chronicles of Narnia*. The others however are older and think they know best. They convince Lucy and themselves Aslan was only a figment of her childish imagination. They ask each other why Aslan would only show himself to Lucy and not them.

The group ends up taking the opposite route to the one Aslan led them to and they get nowhere. They waste a whole day facing things they should never have faced and fighting things they did not need to, all because this was not the path they should have been travelling. Does any of this sound familiar to you? So often in life, the path God leads us down does not look like the easy one. In our own worldly thinking and limited human understanding, God's path often makes no sense to us. People who are seemingly older, wiser and more knowledgeable may advise you to take more logical paths. These are the times you need to hold firm to your God encounter. Godly lifestyle and following the discipleship of Jesus as well as the Bible may grind against the advice of the unbeliever, no matter how much they love you and care for you. They will not understand or believe your God encounters and may deem you foolish, and even childish, for choosing to live life God's way rather than how the rest of the world does things. This is crazy when we step back and think about it, because just look how it works out for us when we try to do it without God.

God's way is counter to the rest of the world's thinking and values, for example, getting married before you move in together and sleep together. Society tells you not to marry until you are older and have experienced life a bit more. Another example is when God tells us to give money (the first fruits, known as our tithe or 10%) to the church, when you are already in your overdraft with bills still to pay. We are also taught to forgive the person who has wronged us, even when they are still causing us problems. Love your enemy. Go to church when the only day off you get is a Sunday and you really want a lie in or to get housework done. Jesus tells us to go the extra mile, serve others and turn the other cheek. The list goes on, but you can see God's ways are so much better than our ways. When we learn to walk on God's paths, He gives us the grace we need and blesses our sacrifices. Even if God asked you to go to the 'front line in war,' so to speak, then it will be the best place you could be, if you are following His Lordship.

God says, *"My thoughts are nothing like your thoughts … And my ways are far beyond anything you could imagine."* in Isaiah 55:8, so we need to get in line with His thoughts and ways.

If you are a young person reading this book, another truth we can learn from this passage is if you have had a "lion encounter" don't let grown-ups play it down. Believe it, remember it and walk the path God is leading you. 1 Timothy 4:12 says, *"Don't let anyone think less of you because you are young. Be an example to all believers in what you say, in the way you live, in your love, your faith, and your purity."*

It is our responsibility to hold on to what God reveals to us and leads us to do. God reveals Himself in different ways to different people. It's often so hard if God reveals something to you, but your mum, dad, husband, wife or friend doesn't believe you, and doubts your "lion encounter". Keep your chin up; if you believe you encountered Him, take the first step to move into it and God will give you grace to do the rest. Having said all this, you should remember to talk though big decisions with your leaders. Be prepared to hold off if they say so, God will bless you in this even if your leader gets it wrong and He will make a way if it is His will. We can get ahead of God sometimes, for example, you know you are called to some sort of leadership ministry in the church, but for this season of your life you might need to be in the background serving tea and coffee or cleaning the toilets. If it is beneath you to serve, it is beneath you to lead. If you are exposed to the stage lights before the light in you is developed, it could consume you and wreck your spiritual walk. Pride is a slippery slope.

Anyway, back to the text. The children end up back where they started after choosing their own direction. Aslan awakens Lucy from her sleep. She tries to explain to Aslan the others would not go the way he led or listen to her. She started to criticise the others, but from deep within Aslan came *"the suggestion of a growl."*

Aslan needs not say anything in response to Lucy defending herself and giving reasons for why she chose not to follow him. After she looks into his face, his presence brings clarity and understanding and even a new strength. She knows she could have followed him on her own accord and all would have gone well. Now, after embracing him in repentance, the smell and love from his mane gives her the strength to do his will.

My prayer is this; pray along with me if you want:

I thank you God, that you have good plans for my life. Give me the strength and grace to do your will. Teach me to be brave in following your commands and will for my life. Thank you, Lord, Amen

Because we are united with Christ, we have received an inheritance from God, for he chose us in advance, and he makes everything work out according to his plan.
Ephesians 1:11

35

The Holy Spirit

The Holy Spirit is our helper, our counsellor and our guide. Without the empowerment of the Holy Spirit, it is impossible to live a Christian life. When you choose to become a Christian, you need to ask the Holy Spirit to fill you. Let Him be your superpower. He will guide you and teach you to follow Jesus and live and do as He has done, and still does.

Grace is being given what we don't deserve, like unmerited favour and blessing. The Bible also teaches us grace empowers us. We are not made righteous or good by our own deeds and actions. Everything in the Christian faith is made possible and accessible through faith in what Jesus has done for us. He paid the price so we don't have to. He died so we can be made righteous and walk in perfect relationship with God.

The Holy Spirit is not Casper the Friendly Ghost; He is a person. He has all the attributes of God, but he is spirit, with no physical body. He is our comforter, guide and the one who empowers us. In John 16:7 Jesus says, *"But in fact, it is best for you that I go away, because if I don't, the Advocate won't come. If I do go away, then I will send him to you."*

One of the benefits of having the Spirit of God living inside us is that we receive the fruits of the Holy Spirit. Galatians 5:22-23 says these fruits are, *"love, joy, peace, patience, kindness, goodness, faithfulness, gentleness, and self-control. There is no law against these things!"*

As well as living in the Spirit, it is important we find a Spirit-filled church and stay there, even when the grass looks greener on the other side. Even when your leader challenges or corrects you. Even when people offend you or when the worship is not up to your standard. The list could go on forever, but ultimately no church or leader is perfect. Remember our leaders will make mistakes, just as we do every day of our lives. My pastor is amazing, but he will always be open about his failings; he knows it is by the grace of God he leads the church. He has sacrificially served in the leading and growing of our church for over 25 years, when deep down he knows it might be a lot easier to have a normal 9-5 job and pursue a career of his choosing rather than his calling from God. It's not always about being a good leader. We as church-goers need to learn what it is to be good followers. We are not just consumers who visit church to receive what we need and then leave again until next week. We should seek to serve in the church, use the gifts God has given us and tithe money into the sustaining of the building, pastor and running the ministry. We may be called to sacrifice time in maintenance, children's work, worship, small groups, social events, stewarding, etc. We must remember that in everything we do, we are ultimately doing it for the audience of one, God. We must not desire to do only the ministry in church that gives us centre stage, but give our all into the things that aren't seen, and sometimes not recognised, in the church ministry.

 When I was young, during one season I remember I was the only teenager in the church. Everyone else had either walked away from faith, moved away or gone to college or uni. Even when our kids were young – and now to a large degree – they are the only teenagers in the church, though there are some children. Phil and I are the youth pastors and for years it has just been us running the kids' work. Other workers have come and gone. We are really grateful for their serving for a season, but in my natural thinking I would constantly think it would be better if we found a church with great kids' and youth work, so our children could have Christian friends of their own age to hang out with. However, although this seems to be sensible and an OK thing to do, I don't believe it is necessarily the right thing to do for us. We need to go where God leads us, stay committed and planted there. Not where we, in our human wisdom, deem to be correct. If God calls you somewhere, that is the best place you can be. Therefore, it is also the best place for your kids to be as well. He knows better than we do what we and our children need, and He will bless, guide and protect you more when you follow His leading. If everyone moved churches because of these sorts of things, then churches would never grow or learn to live in community together. So, I encourage you to listen to God about where He has called you to be and really invest your time, finance and service to make it the best expression of God it can be, in accordance with His guiding hand. You will be far more blessed there and also on the day you go to be with the Lord if you have laid down your life to follow and serve Him where He has put you.

Psalm 84:1 *"How lovely is your dwelling place, O Lord of Heaven's Armies"* and verse 10 says, *"A single day in your courts is better than a thousand anywhere else! I would rather be a gatekeeper in the house of my God than live the good life in the homes of the wicked."*

36

Pride and deception

"For what you see and hear depends a good deal on where you are standing: it also depends on what sort of person you are"
The Magician's Nephew, CS Lewis

In the book *The Magician's Nephew* we meet a peculiar character called Uncle Andrew. By the art of magic, Uncle Andrew finds himself in another world as Aslan is singing it into existence. The children, a cabby, a horse, Uncle Andrew and the witch are all together. It is described as a beautiful scene of awe and creative power. The children, the cabby and the horse love the singing, however, Uncle Andrew and the witch see the scene as horrific. The singing makes them feel a certain way, which they do not like.

Uncle Andrew was full of pride and deception with a hard heart and he managed to deceive himself into believing the worst – when what was happening around him was a creative and beautiful miracle.

When the Lion had first begun singing, long ago when it was still quite dark, he had realised that the noise was a song. And he had disliked the song very much. It made him think and feel things he did not want to think and feel. Then, when the sun rose and he saw that the singer was a lion ("only a lion," as he said to himself) he tried his hardest to make believe that it wasn't singing and never had been singing – only roaring as any lion might in a zoo in our own world. "Of course it can't really have been singing," he thought, "I must have imagined it. I've been letting my nerves get out of order. Who ever heard of a lion singing?" And the longer and more beautifully the Lion sang, the harder Uncle Andrew tried to make himself believe that he could hear nothing but roaring. Now the trouble about trying to make yourself stupider than you really are is that you very often succeed. Uncle Andrew did. He soon did hear nothing but roaring in Aslan's song. Soon he couldn't have heard anything else even if he had wanted to. And when at last the Lion spoke and said, "Narnia, awake," he didn't hear any words: he heard only a snarl.

The Magician's Nephew, CS Lewis

 Uncle Andrew decided his own human understanding and reasoning was superior to the creative miracle that was taking place before his very eyes. He just saw a lot of noisy, dangerous animals. This can be the same for any of us. We can make ourselves not believe, by reason and human intelligence, or by experience preventing us from believing God's power is real. I find it interesting that humans don't like to believe in God's power, like Uncle Andrew. It can make you feel feelings you are unsure what to do with, like guilt and conviction. But so many people will happily see ghosts, mess around with Ouija boards and other dark supernatural activity, believing and remembering it. But when people have a Godly, spiritual, supernatural encounter they will often reason it away, saying it was a childish memory or a figment of their imagination.

 When I was at Bible School, I was a volunteer in a youth café. The place was packed on a Friday night, full of young people, as we gave away free burgers. It was a lovely old building and the doors were made of solid wood, heavy and slightly medieval looking. A large group of young people were messing around on the landing. One young person went into the toilet and a young girl who was messing around ended up having three of her fingers crushed in the hinge of a massive, heavy door. The scene was horrific. The pressure had caused blood to burst through the end of her fingers under the nails, and all three fingers were flat, completely crushed and most definitely broken. I took hold of her hand and covered it in mine in absolute panic. An ambulance was called immediately and the girl was screaming and crying in agony. I cried out to God to heal her. As I was praying, "God please heal her," she stopped crying. We were completely surrounded by about 15 teenagers and they were getting in the way. In that moment, the landing became still and quiet. I looked up into her face, still holding her hand in mine and I realised the pain had gone. All the other youngsters knew this too. I slowly removed my hands from hers, looked down and to my utmost shock I saw her fingers were back to normal and the blood had dried. A reconstructive miracle had taken place before our eyes. We all laughed and thanked God together. The ambulance came and all the youth explained, saying God had healed her. The girl's dad came but he was almost cross he had been called out and he totally didn't believe a word we said.

I hope the girl and all of those young people remember this story for the rest of their lives, but I think the likelihood is her dad would have convinced her it was all a big deal made out of nothing.

"He thinks great folly, child," said Aslan. "This world is bursting with life for these few days because the song with which I called it into life still hangs in the air and rumbles in the ground. It will not be so for long. But I cannot tell that to this old sinner, and I cannot comfort him either; he has made himself unable to hear my voice.

If I spoke to him, he would hear only growlings and roarings. Oh, Adam's sons, how cleverly you defend yourselves against all that might do you good! But I will give him the only gift he is still able to receive."

He bowed his great head rather sadly, and breathed into the magician's terrified face. "Sleep," he said. "Sleep and be separated for some few hours from all the torments you have devised for yourself." Uncle Andrew immediately rolled over with closed eyes and began breathing peacefully.

The Magician's Nephew, CS Lewis

My point in writing this is to say, don't be an Uncle Andrew. Don't deceive yourself and be so full of pride you cannot see the hand of God at work in your life. I find it so sad to read the bit where Aslan says Uncle Andrew can no longer hear his voice and be comforted. Sometimes we can harden our hearts so much to God and His goodness we cannot sense Him or be comforted by Him.

Please take a minute now to check yourself and ask God to soften your heart. Can you dare to believe that maybe, just maybe God is real? And He is a good God with good plans for you? Let Him comfort you right now.

At the end of the chapter, Aslan blesses Uncle Andrew with sleep to separate him from all the torments he brought upon himself. Earlier I wrote that the word FEAR can stand for False Expectations Appearing Real. In Uncle Andrew's case, he thought the animals were going to harm him. This was not the case. Sometimes in life we worry ourselves into a completely irrational way of thinking that we have brought upon ourselves, like Uncle Andrew. We can do the same with all sorts of things. We convince ourselves of the worst-case scenario and before we know it, we think it is actually the case, making

Pride and deception

ourselves ill with worry and fear, when all it is, is a false expectation appearing as if it is real.

For God has not given us a spirit of fear and timidity, but of power, love, and self-discipline.
2 Timothy 1:7

37

Alcoholics Anonymous

Around spring time in 2024 I was finding God was sending several people to me who were struggling with various addictions. It is interesting how God uses us after He has brought us through difficult times and set us free from entrapments like addiction. I started supporting a friend of mine who was struggling with addiction to alcohol and I began attending the local Alcoholics Anonymous (AA) meeting. It was an eye-opening experience for me as I heard many personal stories of how people had fallen into addiction and were trying their hardest to climb out of it. It brought home to me what an awesome miracle God had done in my life to completely remove alcohol and be free from a life of attending meetings, reciting texts and being dependant on other people to stay free from drink.

Through attending AA meetings, I have learned addiction really is an illness. We must therefore treat the substance of alcohol in all its forms as though we are highly allergic to it. We have to stay away from it; we are not the same as other people who can have one or two drinks and walk away. If we were to have a drink we would carry on until we were back in the garden of hell, lying to ourselves that this is the best place to be.

I know some people don't agree with alcohol addiction being classed as a disease, but the Government has declared it to be, because it is something that can kill us. This is why it has a duty to pour money into charities to help people get well. After getting to know my AA family, I have also learned that very much like other illnesses, addiction can run in the family. Often it is evident people with addiction will have addiction in the family, either in their parents or grandparents. I think this could begin to be broken by simply acknowledging we have an addiction and talking about it – call a spade a spade. Then by doing steps 1,2 and 3 of the 12-step programme from Alcoholics Anonymous, which are basically to admit we are powerless over alcohol, realise only a power greater than ourselves (God) can restore us to sanity and make a decision to turn our will and lives over to God. The programme uses the words "higher power" which people can fit with whatever they choose to see as their power, such as a religious figure, mother nature or even a tree. However, I truly believe only God has the power to fully set us free. By admitting out loud, to others and to God, that we have a problem, saying "sorry" and "help me," and surrendering your will to Him this can break the power over your children and your children's children. It is very much as if we have been cursed or put under an evil spell, similar to Edward in the story *The Lion, the Witch and the Wardrobe*, where he has a deep desire/need/hunger/longing for Turkish Delight. Turkish Delight makes him feel sick but still he wants it. The Turkish Delight makes his actions selfish and nasty. The desperate need for it more makes him a liar and a deceiver. Is any of this ringing true for you? I can certainly identify with this during my days with addiction. As CS Lewis puts it:

At last the Turkish Delight was all finished and Edmund was looking very hard at the empty box and wishing that she would ask him whether he would like some more. Probably the Queen knew quite well what he was thinking; for she knew, though Edmund did not, that this was enchanted Turkish Delight and that anyone who had once tasted it would want more and more of it, and

would even, if they were allowed, go on eating it till they killed themselves.
The Lion, the Witch and the Wardrobe, CS Lewis

A quote which resonates within me is from CT Studd:

*"Some want to live within the sound
Of church or chapel bell;
I want to run a rescue shop,
Within a yard of hell."*

I love this quote, and in many ways, this is how Jesus lived. Therefore, He sets an example of how we too are to live. Jesus came to earth for the sick and the needy, not for the ones who think they are well, not in need or good enough as they are, Matthew 9:13. However, Jesus lived in the presence of God, worshipped, went to temple and spent time eating in fellowship with other believers. It's so important to stay in community and be a part of a church family. We need to stay within the sound of the chapel bells, so to speak, if we want to rescue people who are in the garden of hell and stay out of hell ourselves. However, Jesus did not stay in a cosy fellowship. He went out and visited the sick, lonely and desperate people where they were. He brought them out from darkness into His wonderful light.

Since being free from my hell-garden of addiction, I have a desire to run a rescue shop for other addicts. But if I am to do this, I need the Lord and a Christian community to help keep me from temptation. I have been told over the years it is easier to pull down, than lift up. Therefore, it is easier for me to be dragged back down into alcohol than for me to pull people up and out of addiction. I definitely don't want to be pulled back down again, but that's why I need God to do the rescuing and I can just be His mouthpiece here on earth. When I stay close to Him as Jesus did, He will protect me.

If I'm going to help someone who is still in addiction, I need to be wearing my spiritual armour to help rescue that person. Alcohol is still a thorn in my flesh and has a pull on me, although nowadays I also recognise an abuse of alcohol to be the hell it really is. I can step back and see how deceitful and disgusting addiction is and what it does to the victims.

Bill Wilson, the founder of the AA movement in 1934, had a God encounter that set him free from addiction and led him to set up Alcoholics Anonymous. Bill was deeply sorry for his drunken actions one day, and for the harm he had caused to his wife Lois. In desperation he cried out to God. He explains his encounter with God in his book.

"'If there be a God, let Him show Himself!' Suddenly, my room blazed with an indescribably white light. I was seized with an ecstasy beyond description. In my mind I stood upon a mountain, where a great wind blew. A wind, not of air, but of Spirit."

After this encounter, Bill never drank a drop of alcohol again. Bill realised we all need a help from a power "higher than ourselves." We cannot do it alone. Nowadays people are encouraged to seek any greater power but Bill's original hope and intention was to point people to God. I believe it is mainly my God people think they know and seek, but for some their higher power could be Buddha, Mohammed, meditation, the fellowship or the programme itself. But I believe the greatest higher power we can turn ourselves over to is the Power of God, Jesus Christ.

Undone

For Bill's recovery it was all about surrender to God, renouncing of sin, accepting God as Saviour and living a Christian life in earnest. He had help from his friends, Dr Bob and Anne Smith. Together they came up with the 12-step programme, which is an amazing programme that continues to help people stay well and live a life of sobriety across the whole world. I understand the 'higher power' aspect can be anything, but I believe the word of God, and it says in the Bible Jesus is the only way, the truth and the life. So, if you are seeking the God I'm talking about then I can help you. We can't do so called 'good deeds' and expect redemption, salvation, a good life and heaven. We can't give up everything and give to the poor and hope for eternity with God. We can't do any of this without Jesus. Jesus is the key. You can only be saved by surrendering to Him. *"No one can come to the Father except through me,"* John 14:6.

I love the 12 steps of the AA programme and think they hold so much power to set you free from addiction because they are so Biblically based – you can read them yourself online at aa.org/the-twelve-steps.

When I was talking to a friend in addiction, she was saying that she was on the 12-step programme, but didn't know how to pray. In Matthew 6:6-13, Jesus teaches us the outline of how to pray. You will see it is very similar to the 12-step program. Here are a few points drawn from the verses:

Verse 6 – *"go away by yourself"* – find a space where it can be just you and the Lord.

Verse 7 – *"don't babble on"* – you don't need to put on a prayer voice, read out prayers from a book or recite the Hail Marys. Simply just talk. "God I'm here, please talk to me, I'm in trouble, I need help! My life is rubbish!" Be real.

Verse 9 – *"Our Father in heaven, may your name be kept holy"* – He is our Dad, the best Father in the world. So, we respect and honour Him like that.

Verse 10 – *"May your Kingdom come soon. May your will be done"* – His kingdom is His characteristics. He is love, joy, peace, salvation, freedom. In His kingdom (in His character) there is no sickness, addiction, pain, sorrows, depression, anxiety. So yes, Lord let your Kingdom come in my life, in the lives of my partner, children, friends and family. God's will for your life is for you to have a relationship with Him so you can live life knowing your God as your Father; we are His children and therefore we inherit his characteristics. We can live life in joy and freedom.

Verse 11 – *"Give us today the food we need"* – give us what we need.

Verse 12 – *"forgive us our sins"* – repent of your wrong-doings that you know of and ask God to forgive you, *"as we have forgiven those who sin against us"* – this can be a hard one, but if you truly think about all the stuff you have done wrong in thought, word and deed, and how God can forgive you, then we need to learn to forgive others. It is a choice. Choose to forgive and ask God to help you forgive continuously. It will save you from getting bitter and twisted in unforgiveness, which will hurt no-one but yourself. If you ask, I promise God will help you.

Verse 13 – *"And don't let us yield to temptation, but rescue us from the evil one"* – He will help us to fight the desires of our will, which are usually whatever feels good to ourselves in the moment. He will help us to seek Him, so all the ungodly temptations get smaller and smaller. I write more about this in the next chapter.

Undone

This is the blueprint that Jesus has left us on prayer:

1) Take time out to spend alone with God

2) Fix your eyes on him, honour His name

3) Seek his kingdom, Him and His characteristics

4) Ask that His will be done

5) Ask Him for what you need

6) Repent of your wrong doings

7) Forgive others

8) Ask for His help in fighting temptations

38

Lead us not into temptation

In the previous chapter we saw the blueprint that Jesus left us for our prayers. I also want to show you how Jesus teaches us to fight temptation in scripture. If you have a Bible to hand, or use an online Bible, please read the passage where Jesus is tempted in the wilderness, in Matthew 4:1-11.

The devil will question who you are; if he questioned Jesus the Messiah in an accusing way, he will also try it with you and me. Jesus was led into the wilderness by the Holy Spirit to fast and be tempted. Jesus did this not just for us but as us. He was fully human and fully God. It says in verse 2 that He hadn't eaten for 40 days and nights and became very hungry; no kidding! The devil says to him, *"If you are the Son of God, tell these stones to become loaves of bread."* If you are?! Well, He was (and still is) the Son of God and could have changed the stones into bread in a jiffy. This is how the devil talks to us as well. If you are a child of God, then why is this happening to you? If you are set free, why is it so hard? Did God really say ... ? The devil is an accuser and will always make you question the truth of who you are in Christ. Look at Jesus' response and use this as a blueprint for our dealings with the enemy, *"People do not live by bread alone, but by every word that comes from the mouth of God."* He is saying that we don't just need physical food; we need spiritual food as well, and that comes from God.

We can also learn a lot from the second and third temptations the devil throws at Jesus, such as, how to fight temptation in our own lives. It is necessary to point out here the devil actually quotes scripture, but it is always a twisted, half-truth. He makes it sound almost credible and believable, but God will reveal the truth to us. The devil quotes Psalm 91:11 at Jesus, *"He will order his angels to protect you,"* but he fails to finish the scripture, where it talks about his own destruction. It says that He (Jesus) will crush the head of the serpent (the devil). Jesus has already defeated temptation and the works of the devil on our behalf; we have the victory in Christ Jesus. The word of God is powerful. Jesus fights back at the devil using scripture quoted correctly, using the whole truth.

The other day when I was in my local supermarket, I was having a chaotic day. I had too much to do and was feeling like I was spinning too many plates, and it was consuming me. I was only popping in to pick up something to cook for tea that night but as I walked past the alcohol section, there at a stand was a worker who was giving out free sample shots of alcohol. Immediately the devil (wine witch) said to me, "Go ahead, have one. It will help, and no one will ever know." I recognised it as the lies of the devil (or evil powers or even my own flesh) but I also realise in the past I would have taken one and been back off the wagon by the end of the day. I said out loud under my breath, "No it won't help, God will know and I have promised." I defeated temptation by recognising a lie of the devil and speaking out the truth.

It gets easier to recognise the lies of the enemy as we get to know Jesus and His word (the Bible) better. We can only do this by reading the word and listening to God.

In Matthew 6:13 Jesus teaches us to pray, *"And don't let us yield to temptation, but rescue us from the evil one."* God never tempts us, but the real nitty, gritty of temptation is found in a person's heart. It may be a temptation to steal, sleep around, be selfish or lie; for me

Lead us not into temptation

one of my temptations in life is probably always going to be alcohol.

A temptation is a strong urge or desire to do, think or say something we know or believe is wrong. It can be different from one person to the next person. For example, drinking alcohol isn't illegal and it's not wrong. However, for me it is wrong because I have made a commitment to God, myself and those closest to me that I will not drink again. Therefore, it would be wrong to drink again. Please indulge my imagination for a minute to illustrate this point. If I was to go out for dinner with some friends and once seated at our table, the people from the table next to us left a large tip in multiple notes on the table; a £20 and two £10s. All of my friends are good people, but for me maybe the thought crosses my mind to take a bit of the money. My friends would not even have thought about this; it never crossed their minds. I didn't act on the thought, but the temptation was there. Circumstances can be translated into temptation for one person but not for another.

Another more relevant example to me (because I don't actually struggle with stealing money) is when I have guests round for dinner. I often cook dinner in wine and I like to offer guests wine to drink, even though I can't have it. I forget at the end of the evening to give the left-over, open wine bottle to my guests, so it is just sitting there drawing my attention after everyone has gone home. The temptation is there, staring at me from the table. Even when it is safely hidden in the fridge, I can still hear it calling. I must choose to ignore the call of temptation. What stops me? If you are an unsaved alcoholic, all you have is willpower, which is so hard to rely on. But if you are saved it's all by the grace of God, a little willpower, and your promise to God in front of Christian friends and family to not drink alcohol.

This is my point in this chapter; PRAYER. Prayer is the key to overcoming temptation. Not acting on temptation, and – even better – not having the thought in the first place. Over the last year I rarely struggle with these sorts of thoughts and nowadays I can walk down the wine aisle in the supermarket and don't even think twice. It's all a product of my heart and allowing God to lead me. Being a prayerful person will give you a heightened awareness of God. He creates in you a desire to do and think pure things. Philippians 4:8 says, *"Fix your thoughts on what is true, and honourable, and right, and pure, and lovely, and admirable. Think about things that are excellent and worthy of praise."* Jesus is all of those things, and He will help you to ignore and defeat temptations.

If you think about the temptation example I suggested above and think about it from the viewpoint of a person who doesn't pray, I believe the outcome could be a lot different. I fought for years in my own strength and it wasn't enough. Prayerfulness gives us tools to fight temptation, while prayerlessness could mean we open the door to temptation and make foolish life choices that lead to being imprisoned in the trap and sin of temptation. This will put us right back in spiritual chains in the garden of hell.

One more example from scripture is when Jesus is at the Mount of Olives and He asks His disciples to pray while He goes off to pray alone. In Luke 22:46 He says, *"Get up and pray, so that you will not give in to temptation."* Jesus is teaching us and giving us tools to fight and overcome evil in whatever form it takes. Prayerfulness is our armour and our battle strategy.

Lead us not into temptation

As I started regularly going to AA groups, I came to realise the leaders and attendees of AA stress the importance of having a higher power for praying to or meditating on and admitting we can't do it without the higher power. The importance of being sorry and making amends for the things you do wrong and praying for the will of God in your life and the power to carry it out is fundamental to the process. However, AA offers no substantial teaching on how to pray because in theory the higher power can be anything. There is no teaching on how to discover what God's will is or how we can carry it out. It's very inclusive nowadays, so as not to discriminate or offend. I believe this is good to a certain degree as it allows us to follow God freely. It has also enabled many people to access the AA program and following Biblical teaching of Jesus at the same time.

In a nutshell, we admit life is too hard on our own; we need to ask God to help us and save us. We need our heavenly Father to protect us and guide us. Once we have given God the acknowledgement and praise, we can ask Him for the things we need and want in accordance with His will. We need to seek God in order to know His will, and we know His will by getting to know Him. We must reflect on our life and actions and keep a short account with God, saying sorry and asking Him to help us forgive people who hurt us. Just as God has forgiven us for all our short comings, we must learn to forgive others. We must pray God keeps us from temptation and we do this by seeking Him.

In *The Magician's Nephew*, chapter 11, Digory approaches Aslan and is called to account for what he has done. He realises the lion sees the motives of his heart and realises very quickly there is no use in lying.

Undone

When the Lion spoke again, it was not to Digory.

"You see, friends," he said, "that before the new, clean world I gave you is seven hours old, a force of evil has already entered it; waked and brought hither by this Son of Adam." The Beasts, even Strawberry, all turned their eyes on Digory till he felt that he wished the ground would swallow him up. "But do not be cast down," said Aslan, still speaking to the Beasts. "Evil will come of that evil, but it is still a long way off, and I will see to it that the worst falls upon myself."

I believe CS Lewis meant this as representing what Jesus does for us on the cross.

"In the meantime, let us take such order that for many hundred years yet this shall be a merry land in a merry world. And as Adam's race has done the harm, Adam's race shall help to heal it."

By doing the will of God, we can help heal and restore our world to relationship with God. God could just burst in and clean up the mess, but in His sovereignty, He leads and encourages us to do the right thing, to grow and to learn, by His grace and mercy.

Digory is asked to go on a quest to find a tree that bares a seed that will protect Narnia from the witch for hundreds of years. On this journey of obedience to Aslan's request, Digory faces temptations to do the wrong thing many times. At this point Aslan has not promised to heal his mum and Digory is tempted to doubt Aslan's righteous and merciful character, which he experienced when looking into Aslan's eyes. Digory remembers the time when he started to believe the witch's lies – that Aslan was getting Digory to do this just to benefit himself and not for the good of the world Narnia is in.

Lead us not into temptation

The witch is representative of the devil. It says in scripture the devil is the father of lies. He will twist things, manipulate, emotionally blackmail, try to cause confusion and constantly try to make you question God. Did He really say, "You can never drink alcohol again? You're not hurting anyone if you do." This was the same when the witch spoke to Digory. She questions his love for his mother and says things like," *"What has the Lion ever done for you that you should be his slave?"* This is how the devil talks. Everything he says is a lie; his intention is to destroy you and keep you from relationship with God.

On the journey to find this seed, the horse, Digory and Polly have a conversation. Digory and Polly are hungry for supper.

"I'm sure Aslan would have, if you'd asked him," said Fledge. "Wouldn't he know without being asked?" said Polly. "I've no doubt he would," said the Horse (still with his mouth full). "But I've a sort of idea he likes to be asked."

This text shows God wants you to talk with Him. He wants to be in a relationship with you. Yes, He knows your needs but He likes to be asked as this strengthens you and enables you to know His character more.

God does not always give us a map, but will always give us a compass. Spend time with Him.

From left to right – Phil, Max, Gracie and Libby
January 2025

Part Five

Undone

*"Wrong will be right, when Aslan come in sight,
at the sound of his roar, sorrows will be no more.
When he bares his teeth, winter meets its death.
And when he shakes his mane,
we shall have spring again."*
The Lion, the Witch and the Wardrobe, CS Lewis

Epilogue

UNDONE

In the amazing encounter I had with God on the day I made my promise never to drink alcohol again, I wrote a note in my journal. I recorded that in that moment, God did such a number on me I felt UNDONE. It was as if God had unwound me and exposed my innermost parts, and everything was laid bare before Him. I stumbled across a scripture the other day in which the prophet Isaiah cried out before God. Isaiah 6:5 says, *"Woe is me! for I am undone; because I am a man of unclean lips, and I dwell in the midst of a people of unclean lips: for mine eyes have seen the King, the Lord of hosts."* (King James Version)

I have read and heard this scripture before and always seen it as a little heavy. I chose to call my story UNDONE because, as in that passage, it is exactly the word to describe my experience in that moment. It was also exactly what I needed to break the cycle and curse of alcohol addiction that was ruining my life. The prophet in this text felt painfully aware of his sin when faced with God's holiness. He knew he was unworthy to speak the word of God or even to be in His presence. I'm sure, like my experience, it was one of wonder and awe. In that moment God's pure and holy love broke me. I had an awareness that I am unworthy when faced with the creator of the world, but through Jesus dying on the cross for me, I have been made worthy.

You, my friend and reader are worthy – not because you're great, but because of what Jesus has done for you. God loves you and forgives you when you truly repent. Just as you are, He wants you to have a relationship with

Him. He will let you see, feel and know He is the Lord of heaven and earth and at the end of the day, He is worthy to receive all we have.

In his book, *The Magician's Nephew*, CS Lewis shows Aslan singing the world into existence. As I've already mentioned, Aslan represents God the Father in these books. The cabby (a taxi driver from London) who had been caught up in the magic of Aslan's creation says, *"Glory be! I'd ha' been a better man all my life if I'd know there were things like this."* The cabby had been a good man, some might say religious, in the sense he went to church on occasion and did good deeds. But he still wished he lived better. (Just a side note, it is possible to be religious yet still not know God and turn your back on Him. Just look at the priests who sentenced Jesus to death.) In the scene, Aslan's voice is powerful, terrifying and all-consuming. Life appears at every word and sound that comes from him. Light breaks the darkness where he walks.

Then two wonders happened at the same moment. One was that the voice was suddenly joined by the other voices; more voices than you could possibly count. They were in harmony with it, but far higher up the scale: cold, tingling, silvery voices. The second wonder was that the blackness overhead, all at once, was blazing with stars. They didn't come out gently one by one, as they do on a summer evening. One moment there had been nothing but darkness; next moment a thousand, thousand points of light leapt out – single stars, constellations, and planets, brighter and bigger than any in our world. There were no clouds. The new stars and the new voices began at exactly the same time.

The Magician's Nephew, CS Lewis

Undone

I have told you my experience, and now I pray you experience God for yourself. Live a life where you grow in your relationship with Him.

I pray God will help you fight and win the battle of addiction or give you the strength to stand alongside a loved one who is battling addiction.

I pray you will be set free from unforgiveness and pain from your past and your present.

I pray you have a heightened awareness of God living with you.

I pray your eyes will be opened to the truth that although we live in this world, there is such thing as a supernatural world that exists around and in us.

I pray you live with an eternal mind set.

I pray you will grow in the knowledge of what Jesus did for you, in completing the agonising will of His Father and laying His life down to die for you and me.

I pray for you to enjoy life, living for Him and you find His peace.

Amen!

The End

"There's no knowing. But courage, child: we are all between the paws of the true Aslan."

The Last Battle, CS Lewis

For further help

Here are a few recommendations for extra support, especially if you live near Kenilworth, Warwickshire:

Your local Alcoholics Anonymous (AA) meeting can be found using the *Find a meeting* button on the AA website – alcoholics-anonymous.org.uk

If you are looking for a qualified therapist, I can recommend New Hope Counselling. It offers low-cost counselling, running sessions at Kenilworth Methodist Church and online – newhopecounselling.org.uk

The Wellbourne Clinic is a residential centre providing drug and alcohol rehabilitation services in Kenilworth – thewellbourneclinic.co.uk

The Well Christian Healing Centre in Leamington Spa invites people of all ages and backgrounds to receive healing prayer. It is run by an ordained minister in the Church of England – wellhealing.org

You are very welcome to come along to my church, Kenilworth Baptist Church, where I can be found on most Sundays – kenilworthbaptist.church – please come and say hello!

www.ingramcontent.com/pod-product-compliance
Lightning Source LLC
Chambersburg PA
CBHW061747070526
44585CB00025B/2827